"*Dare to Be True* is a heartfelt, faith-driven invitation to embrace identity, purpose, and truth as defined by God, not culture. With raw honesty and wisdom beyond her years, Madison Prewett Troutt encourages readers to trade insecurity and performance for freedom and grace. Her vulnerability and boldness make you feel like you are sitting down with a big sister who loves you too much to let you stay stuck."

—ARIELLE REITSMA, co-host of the *Girls Gone Bible* podcast and co-author of *Out of the Wilderness*

"Madi writes with honesty and biblical depth, offering hope for anyone who feels stuck, ashamed, or overwhelmed. These pages won't just challenge you—they'll lead you toward healing and purpose. If you're ready to live free, this book is a powerful place to begin."

—Bestselling author REBEKAH LYONS, speaker and co-founder of THINQ Media

"Madison Prewett Troutt brings truth with boldness, grace, and a whole lot of heart. *Dare to Be True* feels like a deep breath of fresh air in a world full of confusion and noise. Madi doesn't just talk about truth—she lives it, and she invites you to do the same. This book is honest, practical, and full of hope."

—RILEY GAINES, *USA Today* bestselling author of *Swimming Against the Current*

"Madi is a powerhouse of truth—bold, wise, and unwavering in her call to live and lead with conviction. She doesn't just write about daring to be true; she lives it with courage and consistency. This book is a weapon against the lies that keep us bound, and a lifeline to the freedom found in Jesus. Every sentence points back to Him. Madi is the real deal, and this message will set captives free."

—ANGELA HALILI, co-host of the *Girls Gone Bible* podcast and co-author of *Out of the Wilderness*

"*Dare to Be True* is a challenge to live with authenticity in a world that begs us to perform. Madi doesn't write from a stage; she writes from the middle of real life, and every page reflects the strength she has found in surrender. If you're ready to stop pretending and start living free, this book will be a breakthrough."

—SAVANNAH LaBRANT, YouTuber, influencer, and co-author of *Cole & Sav*

"In a world that is constantly feeding us false information and urging us to follow 'our truth,' we must learn to stand firm in the Absolute Truth of Scripture. In *Dare to Be True*, Madison Prewett Troutt challenges and encourages her readers to break free from what's keeping them bound, and to dare to live in truth and freedom."

—*New York Times* bestselling author JENTEZEN FRANKLIN, senior pastor at Free Chapel

"*Dare to Be True* is an engaging, practical guide to living a life unburdened by worldly lies. This book is both unapologetic and gentle, layering biblical truth with relatable stories that urge readers to live holy lives. As a mom working to raise godly daughters, I'm so grateful resources like this exist!"
—ALLIE BETH STUCKEY, *New York Times* bestselling author of *Toxic Empathy*

"In a world that constantly tries to redefine truth and distort identity, *Dare to Be True* is a timely and needed reminder of who we are in Christ. Through powerful personal stories and unwavering biblical truth, Madi calls us back to the source of our God-given identity and shows us how to stand firm in it."
—TONYA PREWETT, founder of UniteUS and Madi's mom

"*Dare to Be True* is a powerful invitation to step out of deception and into divine truth. Madison Prewett Troutt masterfully guides readers with wisdom, vulnerability, and unwavering faith, making this book a must-read for anyone seeking clarity, confidence, and lasting freedom."
—*New York Times* bestselling author DANIEL G. AMEN, MD

"In a world where it's easy to pretend like everything is okay, I value authenticity and transparency. What I love about *Dare to Be True* is that Madi pulls back the curtain on her life further than she ever has before—and in the midst, points readers back to the only hope we all have for true freedom: Jesus."
—JONATHAN ISAAC, NBA player and founder of the UNITUS apparel brand

"In *Dare to Be True*, Madison Prewett Troutt doesn't shy away from the hard realities—confronting the lies that keep us bound while boldly declaring the truth that sets us free. This is a book for the one who is ready to rise. For those who are done with pretending. For those who know they were made for more."

—*New York Times* bestselling author LISA BEVERE, co-founder of Messenger International

DARE TO BE TRUE

DARE

HOW TO DEFEAT THE LIES THAT BIND YOU

TO BE

AND LIVE OUT THE TRUTH THAT FREES YOU

TRUE

MADISON PREWETT TROUTT

WATERBROOK

WaterBrook
An imprint of the Penguin Random House Christian Publishing Group,
a division of Penguin Random House LLC
1745 Broadway, New York, NY 10019
waterbrookmultnomah.com
penguinrandomhouse.com

Copyright © 2025 by Madison Prewett Troutt

Foreword by Jonathan Pokluda copyright © 2025 by Penguin Random House LLC

LIBRARY OF CONGRESS CATALOGING-IN-PUBLICATION DATA
Names: Prewett Troutt, Madison, author
Title: Dare to be true: how to defeat the lies that bind you and
live out the truth that frees you / Madison Prewett Troutt.
Description: First edition. | New York, NY: WaterBrook, 2025 |
Includes bibliographical references.
Identifiers: LCCN 2025008168 | ISBN 9780593445273 hardcover |
ISBN 9780593445297 ebook
Subjects: LCSH: Truthfulness and falsehood | Christian life
Classification: LCC BJ1421 .P75 2025 | DDC 177/.3—dc23/eng/20250613
LC record available at https://lccn.loc.gov/2025008168

Printed in the United States of America on acid-free paper

1st Printing

First Edition

BOOK TEAM: Production editor: Jocelyn Kiker • Editor: Susan Tjaden •
Managing editor: Julia Wallace • Production manager: Meghan O'Leary •
Copy editor: Jacob Reynold Jones • Proofreaders: Debbie Anderson, Lisa Grimenstein

Book design by Jo Anne Metsch

The authorized representative in the EU for product safety and compliance is Penguin
Random House Ireland, Morrison Chambers, 32 Nassau Street, Dublin D02 YH68, Ireland.
https://eu-contact.penguin.ie

For details on special quantity discounts for bulk purchases, contact
specialmarketscms@penguinrandomhouse.com.

To my daughter, Hosanna Rose,

You are a gift, a reminder of God's faithfulness, and a light in this world. May you grow to know how deeply you are loved, not just by your dad and me, but by the One who formed you with purpose and delight. My deepest hope and prayer is that you would walk unashamedly in the light of God's truth for such a time as this.

This book is for you, my little light. May it guide you to live the life Jesus died to give you—boldly, freely, and full of His love.

FOREWORD

I first met Madison Prewett Troutt—well, technically, I embarrassed her before I met her—when I was preaching at The Porch in Dallas, talking about what not to do when it comes to dating and relationships. In full pastoral fashion, I used *The Bachelor* as a sermon illustration, not realizing that Madi—yes, that Madi—was sitting in the second row, fresh off her time on the show. Everyone in the room turned to look at her. She sank a little in her seat. And I had no idea.

Until I heard about it later . . . and called to ask for her forgiveness.

That call began a friendship that I now consider one of God's great gifts to my family. Madi is the real deal. I don't say that lightly. I've spent decades working with people in ministry—some who wear faith like a brand, others who genuinely bleed it. Madi doesn't just talk about Jesus, she lives like He's worth everything. And He is.

A few years later, our family moved to Waco to serve Harris Creek Baptist Church. As God would have it, so did Madi and her husband, Grant, who had been a part of our team. And ever since, I've had a front-row seat not just to her platform but also to her life—to her marriage, her friendships, her consistency, her obedience. And here's what I've seen: Madi is a warrior. She doesn't flinch in the face of lies. She doesn't follow Jesus halfway. She's all in.

That's why I love this book.

Because Madi doesn't just write truth—she lives it. Every chapter in this book is soaked in Scripture, anchored in conviction, and bursting with clarity. It's bold, but not self-righteous. It's passionate, but not performative. It's full of wisdom—but it's not just head knowledge. It's hard-earned, heart-tested, and Spirit-led.

This book isn't for the half interested or the casually curious. It's for those who know something isn't working. Who feel the ache of striving and still coming up empty. Who are exhausted by the pressure to perform, to please, to pretend. It's for the person who's tired of chasing lies that promise happiness but deliver heartache.

You see, Satan is crafty. He doesn't come at us with obvious evil—he comes dressed in just enough truth to sound right, feel right, and even look like freedom. But it's slavery. Madi knows that. And she's here to help you see it too.

In these pages, you'll be confronted. Encouraged. Equipped. You'll be challenged to trade comfort for conviction. You'll be invited to step out of the fog of cultural confusion and stand in the clarity of God's Word.

She doesn't shy away from the hard topics—sin, shame,

identity, eternity. But she also doesn't leave you there. She points to Jesus again and again. To the freedom only He can give. To the truth that never changes. To the life that's actually worth living.

If you read this book with an open heart and a surrendered spirit, you will not walk away the same. I've seen what happens when someone dares to live by truth. Their life stands out. Their joy holds up. Their faith doesn't flicker when the storms come.

That's Madi.

And that can be you.

So here's my challenge to you: Don't just skim this book. Don't just read it. Wrestle with it. Let it ask you hard questions. Let it press in on your assumptions. Let it pull you deeper into the presence of God.

You were not made to blend in. You were made to be set apart.

You were not made to live in chains. You were made to be free.

You were not made to believe lies. You were made to walk in truth.

Let Madi show you how.

Your life will never be the same.

JONATHAN "JP" POKLUDA
Pastor, Harris Creek Baptist Church,
bestselling author and host of the
Becoming Something podcast

CONTENTS

DARE TO BE TRUE

1

TRUTH ABOUT FEELING BOUND

I nearly blew up our house.

Let me rewind. I married my best friend, Grant Troutt, a few years ago. Our wedding day was dreamy, and our honeymoon was, shall I say *steamy*?! (Well, if you don't count the food poisoning incident, but that's a story for later.) After our blissful honeymoon, we packed our bags and moved into our first home together in Waco, Texas. Neither of us had owned a home before. "This will be so fun!" we said. We were super excited.

And super clueless.

There were so many things we didn't know. We didn't know how to change the water filter on our fridge or the filters on the air-conditioning unit, how to set up auto pay for utilities, or what to do with our terrifying bug problem. Maybe you're judging us right now, and that's okay. I own it: We were ignorant. Or maybe everyone's first home situation is challenging. I don't know. Regardless, it seemed like everything that could go wrong went wrong. We had massive spiders in our house and mice in our garage. The pest control team informed us the spiders were brown recluse spiders. *I'm sorry, sir, WHAT? The ones that can kill you?!* We had mold in our shower that refused to go away. Our drains stopped working and our shower flooded the bathroom. There were cracks in our ceiling. The water was so bad it gave us sensitive teeth and corroded our silverware.

One house problem outweighed them all, and even though we couldn't figure out the cause, it was majorly affecting our health. Grant's symptoms were dizziness, memory loss, fatigue, headaches, and brain fog. I had it easier, with nausea and a mild headache—but those were no picnic either. We were newlyweds, new to the city, starting a new job, and managing a new home. So when we told folks what was happening, several joked, "Welcome to marriage!" This was not what we wanted to hear.

Grant suggested we move into a hotel for a few days because every time we were home, we would feel sick, but as soon as we left the house, we would feel better. We decided to book a few nights at a local hotel so we could think clearly and figure out what to do. Excellent idea! It was like our honeymoon all over again, minus the food poisoning! But as soon as we went back to the house, we felt sick again. A place that was supposed to be our sanctuary had become a danger zone. It seemed to be sucking the life right out of us.

We'd been in our house for six months and had been visited by a seemingly endless parade of service providers: a water specialist, mold specialist, HVAC repairman, and appliance repairman. Then Grant suggested we call a plumber. I thought, *How could a clogged toilet be creating all our health problems?* But since that was the only type of repairman we hadn't yet consulted, I made the call.

The plumber arrived wearing a fully loaded tool belt. He walked around holding an electronic device I'd never seen before. It was like a scene out of *National Treasure*. Grant was on speakerphone since he was at work, and I kept him in the loop on what was happening by asking the plumber questions.

"What is that beeper thing doing, sir?" I asked.

"Checking for gas leaks," he said cryptically. "So far, so good."

A steady, reassuring beep sounded from the plumber's tool. Then he got into our living room and the beeping increased in intensity.

"What does that mean?" I asked.

"There's a gas leak in here somewhere," he said. When he got to the fireplace, the beeper screamed. He turned to me. "Where's your fireplace wall key?" he asked.

"There's a remote with an Off button—is that what you mean?"

"No, that remote turns off the *flame*." He ran his hand along the mantel until he picked up a brass tool. "This key turns off the gas." He demonstrated with a swift turn. "If you don't turn the key, the gas just keeps going."

"Going where?"

"Into the air. Of your house."

My mouth fell open.

"When did you last use the key to turn on the fireplace?"

"When we moved in. Six months ago!"

His eyebrows shot up. "And you haven't turned it off since then? Good thing you didn't light a candle. Could've blown the whole house up."

I had indeed lit a candle. Multiple candles, multiple times. But I kept that part to myself.

How had we not known gas was poisoning us for six months? I asked, "Shouldn't we have been able to smell it?"

"Methane gas is odorless," he explained.

I looked up methane gas poisoning online as he drove away. *Symptoms include brain fog, headaches, nausea, long-term memory loss, and death.* I told Grant what Google said.

"Good thing you called that plumber."

It's kind of a funny story now. We caught it before any long-term harm could be done. The headaches and nausea did go away, and I'm glad the chronic unease, misery, and stress of it all is behind us now.

Grant still won't turn on the fireplace.

But here's the thing: Because we had ongoing sickness symptoms, Grant and I knew something wasn't right in our house. Our bodies needed oxygen, but we were getting toxic fumes instead. Where we were supposed to feel free and safe, we felt sick and stuck.

And it wouldn't have been enough to medicate our symptoms or spend the rest of our lives treating them. We needed to be free from the toxicity. We needed to kill what was killing us. And so do you.

Our entire generation is experiencing ongoing symptoms of sickness. It might not be methane gas–related, but we do wrestle with anxiety, work pressures, mental health struggles, family and relational tension, self-doubt, self-hatred, depression, suicidal ideation, body shame, loneliness, chronic stress, identity and gender confusion, and hopelessness. And then, to cope and numb, we often turn to vices like alcohol, vaping, under- or overeating, social media, binge-watching shows alone, busyness and overworking, shopping, pornography, masturbation, and sex.

The problem is that we often can't identify what is making us sick. We feel bound and powerless, but we don't know why, just like how with this gas leak, Grant and I felt the symptoms and the weight of it but couldn't identify the problem. Maybe you can relate. You feel stuck. You feel like a shell of yourself. You are living with something that is slowly sucking the life right out of you. And you just want to be free.

THAT'S TOXIC

Maybe you can't yet identify the underlying problem you're dealing with, but you can identify symptoms like anxiety, hopelessness, lack of purpose, stress and overwhelm, apathy, depression, or loneliness. Maybe that's what drew you to this book.

We often read books like this because we know God has more for us, and we need change, but deep down we feel like we don't have what it takes. Maybe the reason you chose this book is because you feel bound, broken, confused, or stuck. Maybe you are dissatisfied and defeated, but you know there is more for your life. Maybe this book is in your hands because you are searching for truth and answers. Wherever you find yourself right now, I want you to know that you were made for a life of joy, peace, purpose, and freedom. You can break free from what has been breaking you.

You can break free from what has been breaking you.

Maybe you have made decisions you deeply regret, and you live in deep shame. You feel unclean. Maybe you were taken advantage of by someone you trusted. Maybe you gave your purity to someone you thought would love you. Maybe you had an abortion. Or you have been addicted to pornography, impure thoughts and fantasies, and masturbation. Maybe you have shared naked pictures digitally. Or you've hooked up with someone of the same gender, or you've had thoughts about it. Maybe you hate what you see when you look in the mirror. Maybe you deal with fear and comparison.

I pray that, in this book, you will feel safe and seen. And that you will realize, if you don't already know, there is a better way to live. We don't have to keep living with toxicity. There is a way that leads to hope, confidence, joy, purpose, and freedom. A way that leads to a deeper relationship with Jesus. There is a way that leads to deeper friendships and connections with those you love. A way that leads to greater respect, satisfaction, and love for yourself. If that way hasn't been part of your story up until this point, I pray it's your story by the time you finish the last chapter.

With all the mixed messaging, misinformation, and AI-induced deception in the world today, you may wonder, *What is truth anyway? What is real anymore? What can I even trust?* I don't blame you for wondering. I've felt the same way. My aim in writing this is not to paint false realities or confusing messages that appear to be true and loving, but that only leave you in bondage and deep shame. My goal is to point you to the truth—the truth that leads to a freer you.

If you're looking for a book that tells you what you want to hear, that tells you to follow what feels right for you and ex-cuses your sin, promising freedom but leaving you enslaved, I'll let you know up front that this book is not for you. But if you want to experience unshakable peace, joy, and purpose, to walk out God's will for your life and experience the *more* that you have always longed and hoped for, this book is exactly what you need.

Am I promising you health, wealth, and a life of ease and pleasure? No. But I am promising you freedom—true free-dom, not the kind that feels good in the moment but goes on to enslave you. I'm talking about real freedom—in your mind, in your heart, in your life, in your relationships, and through-out your future.

This book was by far the hardest I've ever written. In fact, I rewrote it twice. During the process, I wanted to quit many times—more than I can count. I felt a heaviness as I wrote, fully experiencing the tension in our world today, the weight we all carry, the questions we have, the lies we believe, and the pressures we face. Most of us feel bound, suffering and stuck, and we don't know why.

One night I was dead asleep, when suddenly I sat up in bed

and wrote in my notebook something God spoke to me. Then I fell back into dreamland. The next morning, I read these words: *The TRUTH everybody needs.*

It hit me in the center of my chest in the *best* way. I knew then I had to persevere to write this book. It wasn't written from an "I'm perfect and I've overcome, now learn from me" mindset. Yes, I've been following Jesus since I was a little girl, but no, I don't have it all figured out. I'm taking it one day at a time as I navigate the good days and the hard ones. This book was birthed from a place of feeling weighed down, from having seasons when I felt stuck, confessing to God and to my friends that I just wanted to be free—free from all the societal pressures I felt, the internal wrestling to be more and do more, the lies in my mind, and the anxieties in my heart. I was breathing in toxic air, but fresh air is what I desperately wanted.

So I started writing from a place of pain and vulnerability. From a place of growth. In the pages that follow, I'm excited to share with you some of what I'm learning. Not only will we talk about what is *true*, but we will also confront the lies that bind us. Then together we will *dare* to walk in freedom, embracing our true identities and living out our God-given purpose.

In the first half of this book, we'll uncover the lies that have been keeping us stuck, and together we will unpack the truths we need in order to break free. In the second half of the book, we'll talk practically about how to overcome the obstacles we will face and the action steps that will lead us to freedom. It's a truth-and-dare process. It takes both faith in the truth and daring to follow that truth with action. With biblical truth and bold, practical steps, you and I can break free from what has been breaking us and live out the abundant life that God has for us.

Remember our gas leak? Once Grant and I discovered the root problem causing all our symptoms of sickness, we *stopped* breathing toxic fumes and immediately felt better! In the next chapter, we'll use our own metaphorical "beeper thing" to discover what's making us feel sick, bound, and stuck, so we can stop living with what is slowly killing us, and we can start living in true freedom and purpose.

TRUTH FOR YOU

You can break free from what is breaking you.

2

TRUTH ABOUT LIES

I have toilet trauma.

How about you? Do you have an irrational fear? Something that haunts you and taunts you and is (perhaps) ridiculous? Well, I am afraid that a snake will attack me while I'm using the bathroom. I think this fear started when a boy in my middle school class showed us a picture of a snake coming out of the hole of a toilet.

And then my irrational fear became a reality the summer of 2012. I was at my great-grandmother's house. We call her Mawmaw. Her house sat in a small town in Alabama called Goodway, right in the middle of cotton fields, with woods and pastures all around. Population was around three hundred, including cows. All the cooking happened upstairs, but downstairs was where we all liked to play. One day I was with my sisters and had to use the bathroom. Since the only one downstairs was next to the back door, that's where I went.

When I stood up after using the toilet, something was by

my foot. And it had eyes. And a forked tongue. *Gulp.* My biggest nightmare was staring back at me: A snake was wrapped around the bottom of the toilet. It was huge, coiling around three times. Its head was just inches behind my foot. I can't even replicate the kind of scream that came out of my mouth. I was suddenly Usain Bolt as I ran wailing to my dad.

He grabbed a shovel and went into the bathroom and . . . well . . . cut off its head.

Apparently, the snake had slithered in through the gap at the bottom of the basement door. That gap got fixed soon enough, but do you think I went back to that bathroom ever again? No way! My irrational fear became real. It happened. I was traumatized. Even now, every time I use a bathroom, I check my surroundings (about five times). Thankfully I didn't get bitten, but I still have nightmares about it.

SNEAKY SNAKE

We've all experienced a snake attack. Not necessarily with a literal limbless reptile in a basement bathroom in rural Alabama, but definitely by that snake known as Satan. His first appearance to humans was in the form of a serpent. A snake. Not only was his physical appearance like a snake then, but his very character is like one today—a slithering, sneaky, scheming, untrustworthy, deceitful enemy, coiled and ready to attack.

What's more, Satan lies. But lying isn't just something he does; it's who he *is.*

So, who is this Satan guy? Let me give you the "Madi summary" version: Satan was an angel—some believe a leader of heavenly worship. Lucifer was his name in heaven, and he was described as beautiful and wise. Created by God and made to worship God, Lucifer decided he wanted to be like God instead. So God cast Lucifer out of heaven, and he took with him a third of the angels—that's a lot of sneaky snakes!

How and why does Satan's fall affect us in the natural world today? Here's how: The Bible calls him various names like "prince of this world" (John 12:31) and "ruler of the kingdom of the air" (Ephesians 2:2). When Satan fell, he didn't fall into a black hole in some other spiritual realm or even into hell like many think. It says in the Bible in Revelation 12:13 that Satan was "hurled to the earth" and in Job 1:7 that he is "roaming throughout the earth."

Lucifer's other names in the Bible are "the evil one" (Matthew 13:19), "a murderer," "a liar," "the father of lies" (John 8:44), "that ancient serpent" (Revelation 20:2), and "accuser of our brothers and sisters" (Revelation 12:10). Yeah, he's bad news bears. But most commonly he is referred to as Satan, the devil, and the enemy. His name in Hebrew literally means "opponent" and "adversary."* He has always opposed God and the people of God. Simply put, he hates us. He hates us because we were made in the image of God, and he hates anything that looks like God or loves God. It says in 1 Peter 5:8, "Your enemy the devil prowls around like a roaring lion looking for someone to devour."

* BibleProject, "The Satan and Demons," *BibleProject*, bibleproject.com /explore/video/satan-demons.

The devil is not some cute, tiny red character with a pitchfork that appears over your left shoulder. No, he is a scheming, evil, crafty, deceptive enemy who wants to take you out. He's a force to be reckoned with. The New Testament refers to Satan over thirty times. Satan has been given a short window of time before he is cast into the lake of fire for eternal damnation (Revelation 12). Unfortunately, he's made it his mission to take you with him.

Satan's attacks are subtle and crafty. We are even told in Scripture that he comes disguised as an "angel of light" (2 Corinthians 11:14). It would be much simpler to identify and defeat the devil if he showed up in red with a pitchfork, twirling his mustache and saying, "I'm here to ruin your life!" But that's not how he works. Satan uses the allurements of the world and the appeal of the flesh to try to get us to do what God commands against. He twists the truth, he tempts us to sin, and then he accuses us.

I don't share this to scare you but to inform you. I want us to be aware of Satan's attacks and know how to fight back so that he won't take more from us. He's coming after our peace, purpose, relationships, joy, salvation, and identity. It can be tempting to believe that the devil has the upper hand in our disheartening world. So, how does Satan scheme? He lies.

Satan tempts us with lies like:

You don't need God . . . you can be your own god.
Freedom and satisfaction are found when you look within.
Sin will give you power and pleasure.
Do what feels good to you . . . God doesn't understand.

God doesn't care about you.

God could never love you after what you have done.

Maybe you can relate to hearing some of those lies or even believing them. I know I can. But—spoiler alert—the devil is a loser. Scripture is clear—in the end God wins, which means that as Christians we win too. Revelation 20:10 tells us "the devil, who deceived them, was thrown into the lake of burning sulfur . . . [and] will be tormented day and night for ever and ever."

Remember how my dad went after the snake in the basement at Mawmaw's with a shovel? The Bible promises that, in the same way, Jesus will "crush" the serpent's head. So that end has already been written. As we say in Alabama, it's all over but the shoutin'.

The victory has been won. Jesus Christ is so much stronger than the devil. In Matthew 28:18, Jesus says, "All authority in heaven and on earth has been given to me."

So, Jesus has won and will win, but the enemy is mad. Revelation 12:12 says that the devil is "filled with fury, because he knows that his time is short." So, he is prowling around, looking for someone to devour. But, in Jesus's name, we can beat Satan.

Sorry-not-sorry about that "spoiler." This is your charge to keep fighting. We can renounce and overcome the lies of the enemy instead of being defined and bound by them. We have authority to declare the truth of God's Word. And that truth brings freedom! Now let's learn together how Satan works. Because before we can go chasing him around with a shovel ready to cut his head off, we first have to learn his strategy.

RUNNING THE SAME PLAY

I love sports.

I grew up playing basketball. My dad was my coach, and my dream as a ten-year-old was to be a WNBA player. It didn't quite work out for me, so instead I'm writing a book on snakes for you. Just kidding.

My high school team was good. We won four out of five state championships during my basketball career. But unfortunately, we lost my senior year. It was the championship game and we had to play a number one seed team, and, I'll be honest, they were better than we were. They were taller and more athletic. The only way we could possibly beat them was if we ran the same play again and again, holding the basketball so they couldn't score.

My dad, our coach, said, "Just don't let them get the ball." So that's what we did. The game started and we got the tip-off, and we just held the ball. If you don't know much about basketball, this is not how you normally play.

We held the ball almost the entire first half. By the second half of the game, the other team had caught on to our plan. They pressured us so intensely that we couldn't keep up the charade any longer. They changed their defense strategy. They got the ball back. And when the clock officially ran out and the game came to an end, we lost.

Guess what? The devil operates in a similar fashion—he runs the same plays over and over. Let's look at the plays he uses, beginning in Genesis, where it all started. You'll see that while the devil is *cunning*, he's *not creative*. We read in Genesis 3:1–5:

Now the serpent was more crafty than any of the wild animals the LORD God had made. He said to the woman, "Did God really say, 'You must not eat from any tree in the garden'?"

The woman said to the serpent, "We may eat fruit from the trees in the garden, but God did say, 'You must not eat fruit from the tree that is in the middle of the garden, and you must not touch it, or you will die.'"

"You will not certainly die," the serpent said to the woman. "For God knows that when you eat from it your eyes will be opened, and you will be like God, knowing good and evil."

If you don't know much about the creation story, let me give you a quick rundown: God made a perfect world. He created the stars, the sky, the ocean, and all the living creatures. Then God made humans in His image. He put the two humans, Adam and Eve, in the Garden of Eden, and they were in charge of working the land and ruling over all the living creatures. Everything was perfect. Adam and Eve had everything they could ever want, a garden to themselves. But they were given one command and warning from God not to "eat from the tree of the knowledge of good and evil" for if they did, they would "certainly die" (Genesis 2:16–17).

Then Satan entered the picture. And I want you to notice the first declaration out of Satan's mouth: a lie. Proving that he is the *author of confusion*. We see from the beginning of time that the lie is core to the devil's character. He's constantly scheming by planting doubts and provoking sin through lies. And his strategy with Eve is his same strategy with you and me. Notice the three deceptions in those verses:

1. *Did God really say?*—He questioned God's character and caused Eve to distrust her knowledge and relationship with God. He says to us, "Would a 'good God' really ask that of you? Is that even what the Bible says? Is that even a sin? Did God really say that?"
2. *You won't die!*—He downplays the danger of sin and calls God a liar. He says, "Sin isn't a big deal. You can do whatever you want, without consequences. God lied to you; you won't actually die."
3. *If you eat this fruit, you will be like God.*—He speaks to the advantages of sin. He says, "Sin is good. Sin is *fun*. Sin will give you everything your soul desires. Power! Pleasure! You can be like God."

Why does Satan tempt us to sin against God? Because Satan himself sinned against God. Do you remember when you were younger and you did something that you knew in your heart was wrong? You didn't want to be the only one caught, so you got your siblings or friends to join you, right? Yeah—the devil does the same thing. He's condemned, so he wants to condemn you. He does that by lying about God's character, tempting you with things that will hurt you, trying to separate you from God, and running the same play—the same strategy of deception—again and again and again.

LIAR, LIAR, PANTS ON FIRE

My mom said she could always tell when I lied as a child because I had a "tell." I would stick my tongue to the side and press it against the inner lining of my mouth. It is as weird as it sounds. That was my body's reaction to lying. I couldn't help it. So, every time I lied, my parents knew. I told on myself! We laugh about it to this day.

The enemy's lies are more subtle. Sadly, he doesn't have a "tell." And his lies can feel like truth. He whispers what he knows you fear. He comes at you, targeting your weakness. He whispers that nobody really knows you. That you don't measure up. That your past defines you. That you don't matter.

Some other common lies Satan tells are:

You will always be what you've done.
You will always be what's been done to you.
You are disgusting. You are dirty.
You don't fit in anywhere.
You will always be anxious.
You are the problem.
You are a burden to everyone.
You are not enough.
You are too much.
Life would be better if you weren't here.

Can you relate to one of these? All of these? You are not alone. In fact, let me ask you a question. Try to answer it honestly: *What lie are you believing right now?* Is it about your looks? Your life? Your future? Your past? God's love and heart for you? Go ahead and write it out.

The LIE I am believing right now is _____

_____.

Want a real picture of the lies he's whispering in my head, even as I write this book? *"Madi, you will never be good enough, no matter how hard you try." "No one cares what you have to say." "Everyone else is so much better than you." "You don't belong. You are so alone." "No one really knows you or cares about you."* At times I've believed those lies. So much so that I almost quit writing this book altogether.

We often treat Satan's lies like they are real. And to be honest, they may even have some truth mixed in. We'll call those lies "half-truths." And though half of something might be true, if it isn't the whole truth, *it isn't true.* Then there are other times a statement is just a full-on lie dressed up like truth. We're going to call that "fake truth."

Here's an example of a half-truth. I used to tell everyone Mandy Moore was my aunt—you know, the actress from the movie *A Walk to Remember* and the TV show *This Is Us.* The truth is, my aunt's name was Mandy Moore before she married my uncle and became a Prewett. She was a southern blonde from Atmore, Alabama, with a kind heart but no acting ability whatsoever. So, I wasn't technically "lying." I just wasn't telling the whole truth. Fake truth, however, is a straight-up lie posing as truth. Like when a four-year-old gets caught with chocolate all over his mouth, but when asked if he's eaten chocolate before dinner responds, "No, Mommy."

Fake truth might be cute on a toddler, but it's not so cute coming from Satan. John 8:44 says about the devil, "There is no truth in him. When he lies, he speaks his native language, for he is a liar and the father of lies." There is no truth in him. Whether that is a half-truth, fake truth, bent truth, or a bald-faced lie, it's all the same with Satan: lies.

Believing these lies creates bondage and suffering. Satan works hard to steal your peace, kill your purpose, and destroy your relationships with God and people. He's a liar. My prayer is that throughout the first half of this book, we identify and confront the devil's lies and schemes and replace them with the truth that sets us free. In this next section let's talk about a universal lie that many in our culture have fallen for today.

"LIVE YOUR TRUTH"

Let me tell you about the time my car got repossessed.

I woke up like normal, made my coffee and breakfast, and was having my quiet time when I was interrupted by my husband shouting, "Madi, your car is gone!" I thought he was pranking me, so I continued with my quiet time. A few moments later he came running in with a panicked look on his face, saying, "It's not out there!" I decided to check out the scene for myself. Sure enough, the driveway was empty. The car was gone.

We looked through our security footage and saw two guys with a tow truck towing my car away at midnight. I thought, *Wow, these thieves came prepared.* But after doing some digging, I realized it was not a thief; it was the repo crew coming to repossess my car.

In my defense, the leasing company had gotten my address wrong and was sending the loan notice to the wrong place, so I never knew the payments weren't going through. I assumed everything was in order and the bill was being paid each month. I thought the car belonged to me. In reality, the car was not being paid for, and now it was the lender's. What I *thought* was true didn't matter. What mattered was what was actually true.

The truth wins every time.

This lie of "live your truth" has been used by the enemy to deceive many in our world today—the idea that if something is true for you, then it's true, period. For example, let's say that "your truth" is that gravity is not real. Even though there is proof and evidence, you "feel like gravity is a lie." Well, if you decide to test your feeling and jump off a building, "your truth" will be painfully confronted with the real truth—gravity will kick in, and the truth will win.

People trying to claim that their truth is reality is not a new problem. The Bible talks about people thousands of years ago who "exchanged the truth about God for a lie, and worshiped and served created things rather than the Creator" (Romans 1:25). And we see that today.

The "live your truth" mindset is often intertwined with New Age spirituality. This teaching believes that there is no absolute right or wrong, no objective truth—just a landscape of experiences that your soul goes through. It gives you false idols to worship, starting with yourself, teaching that you are always perfect the way you are. You are your own god, in a sense.

This mindset encourages you to turn to spiritual rocks and crystals to promote physical, emotional, and spiritual healing. In addition to involvement with crystal power, there are other mystical practices such as astrology, numerology, divination, tarot cards, psychic healing, mediumship, witchcraft, and sorcery.

Why do we worship what's been created, rather than the One who created it? Don't get me wrong, crystals are beautiful, and so are the moon and the stars. But those things are created. They are not the Creator. True power doesn't lie in what has been created, but in the One who created it. God's creation just points back to Him and His power and beauty.

> True power doesn't lie in what has been created,
> but in the One who created it.

It's all just a twist of truth. It's part of how the enemy works as the deceiver. He appeals to a truth that is about you and that serves you. He deceives and lures people in with a "truth" that feels inclusive and loving, a "truth" that excuses our sin and lets us do whatever we want to do. But this "truth" isn't loving. The enemy doesn't love you. He hates you. And he knows that this "truth" leads to bondage.

When we follow culture's lies and mantras on what is true,

eventually "our truth" will be confronted with *the* truth—and *the truth* will always win.

Hopefully by now, you know that you have an enemy. That now you see how believing his half-truths and fake truths—lies—leads to suffering and bondage. The good news is that the slithering reptile is one shovel away from destruction. In the next chapter, we'll see how to find rescue and relief from what has been binding us.

TRUTH FOR YOU

The moment you believe the lie, you empower the liar.
The moment you believe the truth, you defeat the lie.

3

TRUTH ABOUT TRUTH

I almost drowned in the wave pool.

Allow me to explain. When I was growing up, we went to Orange Beach, Alabama, every summer. My favorite part was always going to Waterville amusement park. The smell of coconut suntan oil and chlorine instantly takes me back to memories of the lazy river, the go-carts, the massive waterslides, and, best of all, the iconic wave pool.

One hot summer day at Waterville when I was nine years old, I decided to hit the wave pool, despite it being more crowded than usual. Even with the throngs of people, I was fearless. I grabbed the required yellow ring-shaped inflated tube and spent the first hour kicking and paddling my little feet out to the deeper end. Then the waves would come up and I'd "surf" back to the concrete beach at the shallow end. I started to get a little too confident and would even swim outside of my yellow tube, which was not allowed because some of the waves could be dangerous, especially to a little nine-year-old. But I felt bigger than the waves. Until . . . suddenly a huge wave took me completely by surprise. My inflatable yellow float flew off like a bullet, never to be seen again.

I was underwater.

When I searched for a place to surface, all I saw was endless yellow tubes and kicking legs above me. This yellow wall—or more like a ceiling—kept me down. I couldn't push through and I was desperate. I started seeing stars—like in the cartoons, but for real. I'd never held my breath for so long. I thought, *I'm going to die!*

Then, out of nowhere, an older gentleman reached down and pulled me up onto a tube. My lungs filled with sweet, sweet air as I gasped. Hallelujah!

The man asked if I was okay. I could only nod my head yes. I was so happy I could breathe again.

I think of that story when I read Psalm 40:2. "He lifted me out of the slimy pit . . . he set my feet on a rock." The Madi translation: "You pulled me out of the chlorinated pool and set me on a yellow float." I nearly died, but I got rescued. I was thankful.

The reality is, Jesus saved me from a worse fate. He rescued me from darkness and brought me into the light. He rescued me from lies and brought me into truth. He rescued me from eternal death and gave me eternal life. I was flailing around, unable to breathe, with no hope, until He pulled me up and into His grace and goodness. He took my sinful and selfish choices, hurts, addictions, sins, and anxieties, and He *redeemed me*. He pulled me from death into *life*. And He can for you too.

Even if you've never had a life-or-death experience at a

water park, you can still relate because we have all felt help-less. And if Jesus as Savior still feels a little abstract to you, if you haven't yet recognized your need for rescuing, you will. We were all born falling for Satan's lies and trapped in our own sin. Just like me in that wave pool, we cannot possibly break free in our own strength or power—apart from Jesus.

PRISON BREAK

I am really close to my family, including my two younger sis-ters, Mallory and Mary Mykal. About ten years ago, my fam-ily was obsessed with this show called *Prison Break*. Not to spoil the show in case you haven't seen it, but the whole plot of the show is in the name. It's all about a guy continuously breaking out of prison. Many seasons, he would find himself in a new prison and then somehow break out.

I can't relate to breaking out of prison, but I have broken out of an escape room before with my friends. It was exhila-rating. My younger sister Mary, however, had a real-life expe-rience behind bars during her wild-child stage. (Don't worry, she gave me permission to share this story.)

Mary and I are six years apart, so I was always like her second mama. If she was scared at night and afraid to go downstairs to our mom and dad's room, she would crawl into bed with me. If she needed help with something or needed money and our parents weren't around, I was always the first call.

Although Mary started out as the innocent baby sister, that

didn't last forever. High school came along, and my parents and I would find empty alcohol bottles in the back of her car or vape pens in her pants pockets. There were many conversations with her but no change in her actions. This continued for years. When she went off to college (about two hours away from home), she chose to hang with people who weren't good company, and we grew increasingly concerned. There were a few situations that left us scared, but there was one night that put us all over the edge.

It was 2 A.M. and I awoke to see three missed calls from my mom. I knew something was off, so I called her back. She said, "It's about Mary." My heart started racing.

"Is she okay? What happened? Do I need to fly home?" I was living in Dallas, Texas, at the time, and the rest of my family lived in Alabama. I began asking all the questions in full-on panic.

She explained that she had just gotten off the phone with the police who had arrested Mary. Apparently, Mary was at a college party where she drank too much. And she thought she would drive herself home. Bad idea. Super bad. The worst.

To make a long story short, Mary was pulled over and arrested for drunk driving. The cop told my mom, "If I hadn't stopped her, she never would have made it." I started shaking on the other end of the phone. I was praying in my heart, *Oh Lord, save my sister! Let this be the end of this! Save her, Lord.*

Mary was booked into the county jail that night. There she was, lying on a cold metal bench, alone in her cell, still half-drunk, trying to make sense of what she'd done, feeling the weight of her sin and shame, wondering how she could get herself out. Can you imagine? *How did I get here? How could I do this? Will anyone ever see me the same? How can I face my family and friends? How am I going to get out? Maybe I can call my parents and say, "I promise I'll never do this again and you can have my car and I will drop out of school and waitress until I pay you back. It'll take a few years but . . ."*

Mary looked at the locked cell door. She wasn't going anywhere.

No matter what she said, no matter how much she tried, no matter what she looked like, no matter her greatest efforts, she couldn't get out of jail. She was stuck. Enslaved. Imprisoned.

But she knew the one who could free her. She needed her father to come and pay the price she couldn't pay and bail her out.

Overwhelmed with love and disappointment, my parents drove an hour and a half to pick her up. My dad talked to the officers. He paid Mary's bail. And they released her. He didn't cuss her out. He didn't shame her. He didn't judge her. He embraced her and said, "I love you."

Mary still had to face consequences. She had to stand before a judge and say, "I messed up. I did a dumb thing." She was sentenced and has a police record now. And she had to do a lot of community service. There were some things she needed to work out for sure. But she was free.

That's a picture of you and me because of sin. We are sitting in a prison cell, filled with shame and self-pity, trying to reason our way out, powerless to change our condition. We're stuck.

And even though we can't *Prison Break* our way out of our mess, we know the One who can. We know who can set us *free*.

WHAT IS TRUTH?

One thing I can say for certain about every single human being, no matter their story or upbringing or beliefs, is that we are all searching for truth. We all desire to know what is true. And we all want to be free. Every single one of us. And the two go hand in hand, according to John 8:32.

If you look at our world today with its rise in palm readers, witchcraft, New Age spirituality, astrology, and confusion about our gender, it's all a desperate plea to find truth. That's the thing. We all want hope. Hope that there's more to this life than the burdens and bondage we feel. Hope that there's an escape from the internal wrestling and the imprisonment we feel like we are in. Hope for meaning, purpose, and peace. We're all searching. Only most of us are searching in the wrong places.

As a result, many people believe they are living in *freedom*, yet they are unknowingly enslaved by the very things they pursue. With mass media and social media, AI, secular movies and music, political and government agendas, and news outlets spewing misinformation, there's so much confusion about what is true and real.

We ask questions like, *What is true about me? Where did I come from and why am I here? Where can I find real inner peace, freedom, love,* connection, and contentment? What's the meaning of everything? What happens to everyone after they die? Am I a part of something bigger than myself? Is there a God—one true God? Do heaven and hell really exist? Why does it feel like the world is getting more and more confusing and dark?

We all are asking some form of the question "What is truth?" And we aren't the first to ask. A man named Pilate asked that question two thousand years ago. In John 18, we see the interaction between Pilate and Jesus. Jesus is arrested and brought before Pilate, the Roman governor. Pilate interrogates Jesus, questioning Him about being the King of the Jews. Jesus responds, stating that His kingdom is not of this world and that He came to testify to the truth. Pilate, seemingly confused, asks, "What is truth?" I can imagine that in Pilate's time, just like today, there were many versions of "truth." Many turning to culture, power, idols, money, self, nature, work, and good deeds to find meaning and truth. Sound familiar?

Today, truth is often confused with perspective. Some see truth as a human experience or a feeling. Some think truth is subjective and changes based on a person or circumstance. And I do understand why that is an appealing "truth" to cling to. Because we all want to believe that we are innately good and that our feelings and opinions really matter. Today many believe that if it feels right or seems right for you, then it's true.

But there is a big problem with that belief system: It's not true. A mindset is not *truth*. And because it isn't true, it doesn't lead to real freedom. Actually, it leads to quite the opposite. Like the "freedom of expression" movement that is preached and celebrated today, to follow whatever you feel and express it in a way that makes you feel happy, this type of freedom doesn't free; it binds. Only real truth leads to real freedom. Because truth isn't about you, from you, or based on you. It isn't tied to personal preference, perspective, or feelings.

Only real truth leads to real freedom.

Let me give you an example of what I'm saying. Let's say you or someone you love has a medical emergency like kidney failure and you rush to the hospital and some random lady comes up to you and says, "I can help you!" She doesn't seem like your typical doctor, so you ask her where her credentials are and if she is qualified. She then responds to you, "Well, I am not an actual doctor, but today I feel like being a doctor!" As you question her, you learn that she has no experience or background in medicine. Rather, she just decided today that her truth was that she identified as a doctor. Would you let her take you into surgery? Would you trust her with your life or your loved one's life? I hope your answer is a resounding no. Because believing or following that version of "truth" is not just a ridiculous idea—it could cost you your life. Just because you believe something is true doesn't mean it is. Truth is what actually is, not what we want it to be.

Just because you believe something is true doesn't mean it is. Truth is what actually is, not what we want it to be.

Proverbs 14:12 says, "There is a path before each person that seems right, but it ends in death" (NLT). In other words, just because something seems right doesn't make it true. And the result of following what "seems right or feels right" leads to death.

We live in a time where more information is available than ever, yet confusion about truth is widespread. Fake news, misinformation, and media bias make it difficult to discern reality. Just like Pilate, people are exposed to truth but struggle to accept it. We find ourselves asking, What's real? What's true? About God? About eternity? About me? About my future and purpose? In the search for truth, sadly, most will follow the ways of Romans 1:25: "They exchanged the truth about God for a lie, and worshiped and served created things rather than the Creator—who is forever praised. Amen." Many will turn to stars in the sky, crystals and rocks, and other humans for truth—rather than the God who created it all.

Pilate's story serves as a warning. The world's approach to truth leads to confusion, compromise, and condemnation. But the good news is that there is a better way. There is a truth that leads to breathing in fresh air instead of toxic fumes. A truth that brings color to your life when you've only been seeing black and white. A truth that fully satisfies the deepest longings and desires in your heart. A truth that doesn't lead to confusion but offers certainty, clarity, and eternal life. A truth that sets you free.

Maybe like Pilate, you're asking the question, "What is true?" Pilate wasn't the only one in the Bible who wrestled and longed for truth. In John 14, one of Jesus's disciples,

Thomas, asked, "How can we know the way?" and Jesus answered in John 14:6, "I am the way and the truth and the life. No one comes to the Father except through me." Jesus says, *I am the truth. I am the way.* Our questions and longings are answered, and He addresses not just what truth is but *who* Truth is. Truth is a person—Jesus. And the way to life is through Him.

Jesus was sent to the earth to cancel our debt by paying for it in full with His life. And in His resurrection He disarmed and destroyed all the powers of darkness at work. Jesus was sent not just to rescue us from death but to give us life and life eternal. Jesus was sent not only to defeat the liar, but to be the Truth that sets us free and gives us life.

And it doesn't stop there. Jesus didn't take truth away when He went into heaven. His disciples were a little worried about that, but He promised to send the Holy Spirit. And in the Bible, the Holy Spirit is described as the *Spirit of truth* (John 14:17). In John 16:13 it says that the purpose of the Holy Spirit is to "guide you into all the truth."

So let's make it simple. Jesus is Truth. He came to testify about Himself so that in Him we may know the truth and experience true freedom, life, and life eternal. But then He gave us the Holy Spirit to live inside of us and remind us of the Truth.

So, the question is not as much a matter of "What is truth?" but rather "*Who* is Truth?" And that person is Jesus. And when we find Him, everything changes. Your "truth" will lead you to bondage, but *the* Truth will set you free. You will only be free by the truth—not what you believe to be true.

> You will only be free by the truth—
> not what you believe to be true.

The reality is that we *all* are susceptible to fall for lies rather than live for truth. And though lies may vary from person to person, and each of our circumstances may look different on the outside, we still wrestle with the same things within. And that leads to the same bondage.

You won't find truth by looking within. Because you didn't create you. You won't find truth by looking to culture, because culture is constantly changing. And you won't find truth by looking to what this world has to offer you, because it's fleeting and fading.

"I CAN SAVE MYSELF"

One of my favorite pastors, Jonathan Pokluda, has a sermon illustration about his daughter who fell into the pool when she was little and didn't know how to swim. He saw it all go down from a distance and ran as fast as he could to the rescue! His daughter clearly would have drowned if he hadn't stepped in and saved her. Imagine if, in that moment, she thought to herself, "I shouldn't scream for help. If I can't save myself, I deserve to die."

Although that sounds crazy, one of the biggest lies we believe and the dominant narrative in culture today is that we as humans are so powerful all on our own that we don't need saving outside of ourselves; we think we can save ourselves through our own efforts.

But if we look at the increase in mental health problems, depression, rape, shootings, and suicide in our world today, we discover something quickly: We cannot save ourselves.

For me, I thought my performance, perfect reputation, clean résumé, and good deeds would save me and give me the freedom I longed for. I measured my own worth based on my efforts. If I was good, I deserved good. If I was bad, I deserved bad. This metrics-based system that I put on myself left me constantly striving, exhausted, and feeling like I was never enough. That's because I wasn't meant to save myself, free myself, or sustain myself.

Ephesians 2:3–5 says, "All of us also lived among them at one time, gratifying the cravings of our flesh and following its desires and thoughts. Like the rest, we were by nature deserving of wrath. But because of His great love for us, God, who is rich in mercy, made us alive with Christ even when we were dead in transgressions—it is by grace you have been saved."

The truth is, we were deserving of wrath, without hope, shackled and chained up in our sins and shame, until Jesus. He took our sins and shame—past, present, and future—upon Himself so that we didn't have to carry them. His death and resurrection made it possible to be free in Him. It is by His grace alone we have been saved and set free.

My sister Mary didn't just learn a lesson about not drinking and driving. More important, she experienced a huge demonstration of God's grace. She finally understood what she'd been hearing about the gospel. She 100 percent did not deserve it, but she was given grace. Mary Mykal knew she couldn't save herself. But when she encountered Jesus and His freedom, she was freed from more than physical bondage; she also was freed from the sin and shame that had kept her bound for years.

Her story didn't stop there. One year later, on her one-year anniversary of getting bailed out of jail, she left for Kona, Hawaii, for ministry and missionary training, to be discipled and trained on how to evangelize and bring the same freedom she had experienced to others. She went on to travel the nations to share that truth. She even went to Pakistan in the Middle East and became part of a ministry that freed slaves, paying their bonds and giving them jobs, all while sharing the gospel. She experienced freedom, then went and set other people free, both physically and spiritually.

Jesus doesn't ask you to do all the right things and get all cleaned up to come to Him. *Jesus* did all the right things, took all your uncleanliness upon Himself, and came to you.

Maybe you feel imprisoned in your mind or heart. You feel stuck in the same cycle of sin, trying to change by religion and performance and trying to break free on your own. In the same way that Mary could not get herself free, neither can I. Neither can you. And that is a liberating truth.

Maybe you feel stuck in an internal prison. That was my story. I was stuck in a prison of shame, bound by religion and a slave to sin. Breaking free and finding life didn't feel possible. My truth, my efforts, and my ways couldn't set me free. But just like my sister, I know the Man who could. I know the Man who did. Jesus was the key. He was the key to my freedom. And that can be your story too. Jesus is the Truth that defeats the lie. Jesus is the One who sets us free.

At Waterville, I was saved from drowning by that older gentleman. My sister Mary was set free from her jail cell by our father. Many of us have experienced heroic moments when someone has stepped in and saved us from disaster. But the biggest rescue of all time was when Jesus, Son of God, laid down His life so that in Him we may have life. *We don't have to keep searching and longing and asking, "What is truth?"* Jesus is the Truth. Jesus is the way. And John 8:32 says, when you "know the truth . . . the truth will set you free." You might ask, "Free from what?" Keep reading and you'll see.

In the next chapter, we'll talk about how knowing who Truth is will impact the truth about who *you* are.

TRUTH FOR YOU

Truth is not a personal opinion. Truth is a person.
And when you find Him, you find truth.

4

TRUTH ABOUT YOU

My wedding night was almost ruined.

At the age of twenty-six, I married my best friend. When the wedding night came around, I was a bit nervous, to say the least. I had waited my whole life for this! A big part of my story is that I saved myself for marriage. I made that decision at the age of seventeen as a senior in high school. I held true to that conviction, even though it was hard. (If this is making you a bit uncomfy, don't worry. I'm probably not going where you think I'm going with this.)

After being celebrated at our wedding reception and sent off by our friends and family, Grant and I loaded up into our car and headed to our romantic getaway—the hotel across the street from his parents' house.

After a bit of confusion at the reception desk, we finally got checked in to our amazing room, which was set up just like in the movies—food, champagne, dim lighting, chocolate-covered strawberries, robes, and slippers . . . this was the stuff dreams are made of! We slipped on our robes (in separate rooms because I was so awkward), and Grant turned on some romantic music. My heart was racing.

But first . . . food! We were both so hungry. We'd barely eaten at the wedding with so much beautiful chaos. We sat down to our romantic wedding night meal: burgers and fries. I had just taken my first bite when the hotel phone rang. Grant paused the music and answered it.

"Mr. Troutt, we don't have your card on file at the front desk. Can you confirm that number?" Grant hurried to give his card info so that we could get back to our romantic wedding night. He hung up and hit Play to resume our playlist. Not two bites later, we heard a knock on the door. We looked at each other like, *You have got to be kidding! What is happening?*

The woman from the hotel front desk greeted us apologetically. "So sorry. I've gotten multiple calls from your family, so I finally put them through on the hotel phone. Is everything okay?"

We looked at her, confused. Grant said, "We haven't talked to them. But we did just get a call from you asking for our credit card number."

I had a sinking feeling when I saw her sudden look of concern. She said, "That was not me!"

We looked at each other and Grant said, "*What?* Okay, we will figure this out," and closed the door.

It turns out that someone had called the front desk multiple times, pretending to be our family. When they finally were put through to our room, they then fooled *us* into thinking they were the hotel front desk. After all, who else would call us on the hotel phone? We immediately realized that stranger now had our credit card information, house address, and hotel room number. We felt violated, vulnerable, and unsafe.

Grant tried calling the bank to cancel our card and couldn't get through right away. He paced and talked through possible scenarios, strategizing and planning. I was near tears. I thought to myself, *This is not how I imagined my wedding night!*

Hours later, we got in touch with the bank, and they were able to cancel the card. Our wedding night was off to a rocky start, but thankfully we got it straightened out and were finally able to enjoy it in a much better way.

It's funny to talk about this deception now, but at the time it was so *not* funny. Someone had schemed and lied to take what belonged to us. While that thief was caught, I am reminded of a very real enemy who wants to steal what belongs to you: your true identity—who God created you to be. He wants to create chaos and crisis in your life. He wants you to question God. And yourself.

However, your identity in Christ is not his to take. My prayer for you is that you'd walk in the awareness that hope belongs to you. Let's first identify the lies about your identity so we can take back the truth about who you really are.

UNDERSTAND THE UNTRUTHS

There was a viral video years ago that circled the internet. It showed a guy named Antoine Dodson talking about how a stranger broke into his sister's room and crawled into bed with her while she was sleeping. He heard her scream and came to her rescue. Thankfully, she was okay, and the guy ran off. But the brother went on to talk to the news about the wild world we live in today, and he left us with the viral statement, "Hide yo' kids, hide yo' wife, and hide yo' husband." This video sadly did not serve as the warning it intended—for everyone to secure their homes and be on guard—as much as it served as a meme and a silly audio that turned into some type of jingle.

Even though this is a funny video on the web today, I do think there is some truth in it. We have a thief and a murderer on the loose, and his name is Satan. He comes to steal our identity and kill our intimacy. Although we are not to be afraid, we are to be on guard and know how we can fight back to protect what rightfully belongs to us.

Although Satan isn't physically crawling into your windows to hurt you or even calling your hotel phones on your honeymoon to take your money, there is something he wants to steal: your true God-given identity. And Satan uses the tools and resources in culture to constantly propagate lies about who you are. He's an identity thief! Let's look at two common lies he tempts us with.

1. "It's best to follow your heart and do what makes you happy."

Want to know the trending memes and quotes that I am seeing right now as I write this book?

- "You do you, boo-boo."
- "Listen to your inner voice."
- "Do whatever makes you happy."
- "Choose you over everyone else."
- "Your heart knows the way."

At first glance, culture's message of "Follow your heart! Trust your feelings" *sounds* like good advice. I mean, if you *feel* something, it's got to mean something, right? Shouldn't you choose yourself first, even at the expense of others, since you must protect yourself? I mean, you should be able to trust your own heart, even if you can't trust anyone else—right?

Well, *no*. Jeremiah 17:9 says, "The heart is deceitful above all things and beyond cure. Who can understand it?" We actually can't trust our hearts and feelings because they will lie to us. To really know who we are and to walk confidently in who we were created to be, we must not live based off what we feel, but rather off what is *true*.

2. "Self-love is the real love."

The problem is that self-love is all about self and it quickly turns to self-obsession. As a society, we are consumed with self. The word "selfie" was even added to the Merriam-Webster dictionary in 2014 because so many people started taking pictures of themselves and posting them online.

What are some of the affirmations that self-lovers cling to?

- "I love and accept myself unconditionally."
- "I let go of what no longer serves me."
- "Everything I want, wants me back."
- "I attract what I want."
- "My presence holds power!"

Even if these aren't the mantras you are clinging to, think about how often you focus on yourself. We walk into a room and wonder what other people are thinking about us. We do kind things for others hoping to have them say nice things to us or to give us something in return. We only like a group picture if we think we look good in it.

Scripture talks about this love of self in 2 Timothy 3:1–5, cautioning that it's one sign of the end times:

> There will be terrible times in the last days. *People will be lovers of themselves,* lovers of money, boastful, proud, abusive, disobedient to their parents, ungrateful, unholy, without love, unforgiving, slanderous, without self-control, brutal, not lovers of the good, treacherous, rash, conceited, lovers of pleasure rather than lovers of God—having a form of godliness but denying its power. Have nothing to do with such people.

That's sobering, isn't it?

Satan says that self-love is real love. But the Bible—the Word of Truth—associates this "loving of self" as being ungodly and of the world, commissioning believers to have nothing to do with loving ourselves. Rather, as followers of Truth, we should instead "die to ourselves." Jesus shows us that self-love is not real love, nor is it how you "find yourself." Jesus says in Matthew 10:39, "Whoever finds their life will lose it, and whoever loses their life for my sake will find it."

Here's the Madi translation: Jesus said, "If you want to be my disciple, you don't pamper yourself. You don't put yourself first. Stop thinking about yourself and instead make your life about how you can serve others."

We didn't create ourselves; therefore, we can't find what we need in ourselves. We didn't create the world; therefore, we can't attract and command what we want from the world. There is only One who created you and me. And His name is Love. His name is Life. And in Him alone is love found and real life lived.

You can't self-love yourself into happiness. And you can't self-care your way into meaningful relationships or daily purpose or inner peace. Self-love is always about self and is therefore self*ish*.

The truth is that living for self enslaves you. Following passion and pleasure imprisons you. You can't find what you want deep down within yourself. Only something outside of you, only something greater than you—like the One who created you—can give you what you really desire.

The "you be you" mentality only creates more confusion and insecurity. The "I can do anything I want" attitude only brings anxiety and frustration. *If you want to change your gender, change it! If you want to change your sexuality, change it! If you want to change your pronouns, change them!* That is not real freedom, that is bondage. That is not "living your truth," it is living a lie. We were created intentionally and purposefully, with the looks we have, gender we have, and sexuality we have.

I understand that the way we have been raised often has an impact on how we view ourselves and what we believe to be true about life. I realize that some people have been hurt, rejected, and abused so badly that they believe the only way to be loved and accepted is to change themselves from who they were designed to be. If you fall into that category, I am sorry for what has been done to you, spoken over you, or demanded of you. I don't know your past or your pain, but I know the One who can use it all for a greater purpose than we could ever imagine.

For me, I was blessed to grow up in a Christian home with parents who loved God and loved me. They raised me to know Jesus and to know who I am. And I did—at least for a while. Then when I got to high school, I became confused with who I was. I will share more of my story and my own search for truth throughout this book, but I want to say here that there were many moments throughout my life when I felt "not good enough" and "unclean and unforgiveable." After getting rejected by my first love, falling into sexual and secret sin, and getting picked on and made fun of by mean girls, I often put labels on myself that were untrue.

So I would turn to boys, to sports and awards, to attention and followers, to having a perfect reputation to define me. But I never felt satisfied or even secure. I felt like I was on a never-ending roller coaster. One day I would feel good about myself, and the next day I would hate myself.

That's because if my sense of self is rooted in me, I am the one who must sustain it. Our identities were never meant to be in the hands of someone imperfect, someone whose feelings change every day. The enemy wants you to place your identity in everything but God. And Satan will seduce you with lies, in what seems true, only to deceive you and take from you. The enemy wants you to trade in your true identity for a fake one, because he is terrified of what will happen when you discover who you really are and who you were made to be.

YOUR REAL ID

I never had a fake ID, but I've seen my fair share of them. It seemed like everyone had fake IDs in senior year of high school and freshman year of college. I was always amazed they didn't get caught, because often the picture looks wildly different from the person carrying it, or the information is so obviously random. Grant's fake ID said his address was "1928 Whiskey Road." Like, come on! The ID never seems to line up with the truth of the person carrying it. Why? Because it's *fake*!

Many of us today are living with fake IDs of a different sort. Your fake ID has false information, like the enemy's lies about who you are or old information about who you used to be. But why carry around a fake ID when you can have a real, true one? One that can get you into the best party of all time (heaven) when a fake ID can't. One that gives you the confidence to stop looking over your shoulder or wondering if you're going to get caught. One that gives you the real security you crave and the answers to who you really are. One that will give you the strength, grace, and courage to become all you were meant to be.

Perhaps you have believed lies about yourself for so long they feel like truth. Perhaps you have allowed something you did to define you. Perhaps you struggle with your identity because you are so consumed with someone else's "perfect" identity. Perhaps you don't know how to feel secure in who you are because everything around you feels so unstable. Or perhaps you have allowed the words and comments of other people to tell you who you are.

Let me be real with you about my struggle with identity. You may think because I wrote this book or have quite a few social media followers that I somehow have my stuff together. I opened up to you about my wrestling with who I was in high school. But it didn't stop there. It's been a fight my whole life.

When I entered college, I decided to do sorority life. I was so excited because all my friends were going through rush (the process to get into a sorority) with me. I went in with my 4.0 GPA, all my success in school and sports, and my long list of letters of recommendation. I was sure I would get the sororities I wanted. But by the end of rush week, I found out that all my top sororities had dropped me. What made it harder is that none of my friends got dropped, and they all got the sororities they wanted. I wondered, *What is wrong with me? Why am I so unpickable?* Because of that rejection, I questioned my identity and didn't feel good enough.

The insecurity continued even after I graduated. I had

been dating a guy for four years, all throughout college. After graduation, we knew it was time to start talking about engagement. But after much prayer, I felt God ask me to give up that relationship to Him. I said no for a long time. I finally agreed to give God the relationship, fully believing that after He taught me whatever lesson He wanted to teach me, I would get the relationship back. But it didn't quite go as I had hoped. We broke up, and just a few months later, I found out he was already dating someone else. And that someone was my best friend. *Ugh, that hurts.* It was a deep sting of betrayal, with two people I had loved. My identity felt shattered for a while.

When I was twenty-three, I went on a reality TV show called *The Bachelor.* And let me just say, that experience is not for the faint of heart. Throughout filming that season, my identity and faith were tested. But the hardest part for me was when the show aired. I went from anonymous to millions of followers—with opinions—overnight. Tens of thousands of DMs, comments, news articles, and podcasts about my looks, my accent, my character, my convictions, and my family. Although many of the opinions about my faith and personality were positive, there were lots of mean and hateful comments. It got to me. I lost over twenty pounds. I felt anxious all the time. I questioned who I was because of what other people said about me. My identity, at times, felt lost.

Even later, when Grant and I first got married, I struggled with my identity for a while. Something about changing my last name and adding the title "Mrs." created a bit of an identity crisis I wasn't expecting. Although I was so excited to be married to the love of my life, I also grieved who I once was and the single life I once lived. I wondered, *Was I made for this? Can I even be a godly wife?* My identity felt confused.

When Grant and I got pregnant with our baby girl, as thankful and excited as I was, I started to feel these same feelings arise again. *My life is changing. I am gaining another title: Mama.* I questioned, *Do I have what it takes to be a godly mom? To raise godly kids?* I also watched as my body began to change, and that was something I couldn't have prepared my mind for. A growing belly created insecurity that I wasn't expecting. I didn't want to leave my house because I couldn't fit into any of my clothes, and I didn't feel like I looked like myself. I couldn't keep up and do as much as I did before. I was tired all the time. I even found myself struggling with comparison on social media and seeing everyone else in their perfect pregnant era. They had the perfect bump, with the cutest outfits, and the nursery all done and ready months in advance. Meanwhile, I felt like a whale, and Grant and I were living in an apartment while looking for a house, and boxes were everywhere.

As you can see, I have wrestled with my identity again and again. And the truth is I will wrestle with it again. There will always be the temptation to carry around a fake ID and believe the lies of the enemy about who I really am.

But when we feel the weight of the lies, we have to fight to remember the truth. In each of those seasons of my life as I struggled to be confident in who God made me to be, I would turn to Scripture to remind me of the truth. Or I'd call a friend to pray over me and speak God's truth to me.

Because the truth is that when we believe in Jesus, our fake ID gets thrown out, and our new ID is given. We are no longer defined by our mistakes. We are no longer bound by what other people think about us. We are no longer a slave to sin. We aren't limited to the labels of this world. We aren't stuck in the enemy's lies. With our real ID—who Jesus says we are—we are set free.

No matter what lies you have believed or things you have done up until this point, the good news is that Jesus Christ comes to redeem. And He rewrites stories. He redeemed and renewed me, washing me clean and giving me my true identity. He removed the guilt and shame I had been wearing and the lies I had been believing. He clothed me in His love, His light, and His truth.

Letting the One who created me be the one who defines me is the greatest decision I have made. It is no longer my shortcomings, failures, sins, or struggles that define me. The old me is dead and gone.

Jesus comes to make you new too, no matter your past or current struggles. If you give your heart to Him, He will wash it clean—just as it says in 2 Corinthians 5:17: "Therefore, if anyone is in Christ, the new creation has come: The old has gone, the new is here!"

We were all created in the image of God. And since we are made in His image, it's important that we know who He is. If we don't know who He is, or don't have a right view of who He is, we'll always be confused about who we are. We cannot walk in our identity apart from Him.

We don't have to carry around a fake ID or an old ID, for we have been given a *real* one, a new one. We are now sons and daughters—not to be enslaved to sin again or confused by the lies of the world about who we are. We are to remember and walk in our sonship as daughters of the King. We overcome lies when we know the truth of who we *really* are.

Remember the story about someone interrupting our wedding night by trying to steal our credit card? You know what would've been really crazy? If Grant and I found out someone stole our identity information and money and just said, "Oh, well. It's just a thief! We'll figure it out one day . . ."

If you found out someone stole your actual identity, and they were walking around pretending to be you and stealing your money, you would do something about it immediately.

The enemy comes to steal our identity in Christ—to steal the abundant life Jesus promised—and it's time to do something. It's time to take back what's ours. To fight for what belongs to us. To know who we were created to be—and what was freely given to us at a tremendous cost: our true identity.

TRUTH FOR YOU

When you know whose you are, you will know who you are.
Your identity has less to do with you and more
to do with the One who created you.

5

TRUTH ABOUT SIN

"Swim at your own risk."

My best friends and I got to the beach and saw double red flags whipping around next to the lifeguard's chair. We knew that meant no playing or swimming in the ocean. The intense wind was making the waters too rough. There was only one lifeguard on duty, and it was his responsibility to make sure no one got in the water. He had his work cut out for him because the beach was very crowded and apparently full of risk-takers. My friends and I watched as this one lifeguard ran up and down the beach telling people to get out of the water. As soon as he made his way down the beach to the next group of people, others got in the water, and he had to run up the beach and politely urge them out again. I could see the stress on this poor guy's face.

As the lifeguard ran up and down the beach urging the people out, no one seemed to care that he was shouting about the dangers of the water or that the double red flags were flying. They listened to his warning, then chose to ignore him and go out into the dangerous water anyway. Finally, after lots of running back and forth, he made his way up the lifeguard stand. At the top, he yelled through a megaphone: "Please get out of the water! Stay out of the water. All of you! I know it looks fun, but it is dangerous, and it could kill you! I'm not trying to ruin your day. I'm trying to save your life!" He pleaded with such desperation and conviction that it finally got everyone's attention.

In that moment it was like the Holy Spirit spoke to me: "That is a picture of sin." What we couldn't see on the beach were the powerful currents beneath the water. On the surface, the ocean seemed safe. But below, it had the power to kill.

Sin lures you in. At first it looks fun. And maybe it *is* fun, like when you're at the ocean and step in, and the water feels nice. You are only ankle deep and you feel in complete control. Then you inch forward until you're waist deep. The weight of the waves and the current increases, but you're not worried. Even though you are feeling the pressures of the water, you still think you can manage it. Plus, you see everyone else around you in the water too. So you go a little deeper, and now you can't touch the bottom. The waves that were once fun and freeing now take you by surprise. Soon you're no longer in control.

That lifeguard knew something the people didn't. It only takes one wave to knock you down, suck you in, trap you, and cost you your life. The lifeguard warned people about the danger of the water not because he wanted to keep them from fun, but because he valued their lives.

In the same way, sin lures you in. It promises pleasure, happiness, and freedom. And at first, you may feel those things. But the longer you stay and the deeper you go, it ends up costing you way more than you were willing to pay. Sin's price is death. It is not to be toyed with or tolerated. You can't make friends with sin or ignore sin and expect to escape its consequences. It may start off fun when you feel in control. But sin is stronger than you, just like the ocean. You can't manage or control it. It manages and controls you.

Let me be that lifeguard right now that waves my hands around, blowing my whistle, pleading with you to stay out of sin. It will cost you everything. And just like the lifeguard, I care about your survival and want you to experience life, true life.

BORN THIS WAY

Lady Gaga used to be one of my favorite artists. I even had a Lady Gaga–themed birthday party. I loved her—until she dressed up covered in raw meat at one of those famous people's award shows. She came out with a popular song over ten years ago called "Born This Way." Although her implied message is one of "self-liberation" and "self-expression," like much of the messaging today that is ungodly and untruthful, there is a message we can take from the song when it comes to sin—because we are all born with a sin nature. So when there are arguments about being born attracted to the same sex, I would say, "And I was born selfish, prideful, angry, with a thirst for power and control." The point is, we are all born with sin. That's why Jesus came and died and rose again—so that we didn't have to be slaves to that sin.

So, what is sin? Sin is when we break God's law. The Hebrew meaning of "sin" is "to miss the mark."* Sin isn't just bad actions. It starts with our minds. Our outward actions only mirror our inner condition. To sin is to miss the target of God's standards—or even to rebel, reject, or ignore them. It's the opposite of righteousness. If righteousness is living within God's just and right standards, sin is failing or refusing to live by them.

Our outward actions only mirror our inner condition.

Maybe you are wondering, *Why does God let sin exist, then?* To be clear, God did not create sin. The Bible says that God is the Creator of all things good (James 1:17). "God is light" and "in him there is no darkness at all" (1 John 1:5). God created a good universe and good human beings. The Bible reminds us of this truth in 1 John 2:16, "For everything in the world—the lust of the flesh, the lust of the eyes, and the pride of life—comes not from the Father but from the world." Which means that sin is not original. There was a time when there was no sin. Satan was the first sinner, like we talked about in chapter two, and then he tempted Adam and Eve in the Garden of Eden to sin. After that, the rest of humanity followed. That's where you and I come in.

* BibleProject, "Khata—Sin," *BibleProject,* bibleproject.com/explore/video/khata-sin.

Many believe that we are born perfect and good until we sin, implying that the world is the problem and we are perfect until the world corrupts us. That is a lie. The world is a problem, but apart from Christ so are we. The Bible speaks very clearly that we are born into sin with a sin nature. Psalm 51:5 says, "For I was born a sinner—yes, from the moment my mother conceived me" (NLT).

If we look at a child and their natural instincts, we see their sin nature from the start. Just ask my parents—I was a strong-willed kid who wanted my way. I was stubborn, rebellious, and headstrong. I often got disciplined with many spankings from my parents and frowny faces from my teachers. My mom told me about a time when I was around three years old and we were out shopping at the mall, and she said it was time to go. I didn't want to go home and nap; I wanted to stay and shop! So I decided to throw a temper tantrum. I ripped her earrings right out of her ear and proceeded to scream bloody murder while kicking and flailing my body all around. All because I didn't get my way. Now you understand the abundance of spankings.

The reality is, we all came into this world with a sin problem. Why do you think a lot of kids' favorite words are "no" and "mine!" Take my story, for example. A kid has no problem selfishly screaming and throwing temper tantrums just to get her way, even if it hurts the people around her or is disobedient to her parents. Thankfully, I have matured since that embarrassing little three-year-old version of myself—though Grant might argue that I still have occasional temper tantrums.

We come into this world naked, but we come clothed in

sin. Romans 5:12 says, "Therefore, just as sin came into the world through one man, and death through sin, and so death spread to all men because all sinned" (ESV). We come into this world clothed in sin as much as skin. So, whether you grew up attending church your whole life or to this day don't know how you feel about God, one thing is for sure: We have all sinned. We have all been or are currently stuck in sin. We came into the world with a sin problem. And that sin problem just keeps on growing, until we find the God solution.

Until we accept the free gift of Jesus, the payment for our sins, we will continue to be stuck and enslaved in sin.

"SIN IS NO BIG DEAL. EVERYONE DOES IT!"

I love the *Lord of the Rings* movies. Grant and I watched all three of them on our honeymoon. (*Romantic, right?* I told you, I got food poisoning!) If you haven't seen the movies, I'm going to try my best not to ruin them too much for you.

The *Lord of the Rings* series is good versus evil, a fight to destroy an evil spirit that has manifested in a ring. This ring has power. In the film you see an intense love/hate relationship with the ring. Whoever has the ring feels heaviness and depression. It begins to change them for the worse, yet they are drawn to it and desire it because of its power.

When I watch the movies, I see this beautiful gold ring representing sin. It's alluring, attractive, and seems good. A character named Gollum is lured in by the ring, and part of him desperately and deeply desires it. But the ring leads him to isolation and madness, and to eventually forgetting who he truly is. His appearance changes. His name changes. And he lives in caves and eats like the wild animals. He hates what the ring does to him and who it makes him be, yet he feels enslaved to it.

You and I have a similar battle with sin. We are drawn to it because it looks good or feels good in the moment. Part of us wants it. But when we fall for it, we feel the gravity of its consequences almost immediately. Sin enslaves us and begins to kill us.

One lie that Satan has tried to deceive us with is that sin is not a big deal. He makes us believe that sin won't cost us anything. And maybe at first it doesn't. So we keep doing it. We continue in sin because we have the desire and fall for the lie, but as we get deeper in sin we see the danger: that it's deadly. It kills our intimacy with Jesus. It destroys our joy and our God-given purpose. Sin starts as a desire but leads to death.

Some of us think we can manage or tolerate sin, saying, "I've got it under control!" But John 8:34 says, "Everyone who practices sin is a slave to sin" (ESV). And Romans 6:16 says, "Don't you realize that you become the slave of whatever you choose to obey? You can be a slave to sin, which leads to death, or you can choose to obey God, which leads to righteous living" (NLT). You cannot manage sin, just like you cannot manage the stormy waves.

If you don't master sin, it will master you. You'll be bound to what you obey. Many of us flirt with sin but then wonder why we fall into it. Sin cannot be flirted with; it must be fled from.

Sin cannot be flirted with; it must be fled from.

Even if we circle all the way back to Adam and Eve when they sinned in the garden, notice that what was promised by the sneaky snake was freedom, power, satisfaction, knowledge, and goodness. Yet that was *not* what followed their sin. It was shame, darkness, isolation, separation, and a curse. *This* is where strongholds began. Sin didn't lead to superpower; sin led to slavery. Sin is serious and it has ripple effects, including creating generational strongholds. *Your sin doesn't affect just you but those around you and those who come after you, until you cut it off.*

What sin are you carrying that's weighing you down right now? Is it living for the approval of people? Is it obsession with money and status? An addiction or dependence on alcohol? Addiction to masturbation? Jealousy and envy? Bitterness and unforgiveness? For me in high school it was people pleasing, pornography, and masturbation. In college, it was pride and control. In my early young adult years, it was fear, comparison, doubt, and jealousy. And as I write this book, I still wrestle with pride, people pleasing, and apathy. Unlike the lies that Satan speaks, saying that sin "isn't a big deal," now we know that sin enslaves us. And it doesn't just go away when left ignored and undealt with. It spreads.

SMALL SINS SPREAD

There was a bad drought in Waco the first year we lived there. In fact, it was the worst drought in hundreds of years. There were fines for watering your grass, so we had to be okay with our grass looking like straw. Because we couldn't give our lawn the water it needed, something interesting happened. Weeds began to grow. They grew everywhere, spreading like wildfire. From afar it appeared we had green grass—until you got up close and saw a bunch of dead grass and ugly weeds.

Sin and weeds have a lot in common. In the same way that weeds produce tiny little seeds that cause them to spread quickly, sin has a rippling, compounding effect. Sin produces more sin. One sin leads to another and then another.

Just like wading into dangerous ocean water seems okay at first, sin starts small. It starts with one drink, one lie, one pill, one website click. And sin doesn't just come out of nowhere. It usually starts with a thought or a feeling. Sin is conceived when our minds ingest ideas. So ask yourself, *What am I consuming? What movies and shows am I watching? Who am I following on social media? What are my friends like?* These things will impact our thought life and what goes into our hearts, which will impact how we live.

And sin may start "small" in our minds, but it never stays small. It may start as one lie, one photo, one puff, one drink, but if it isn't cut off or replaced, it won't stop there. It will spread like those weeds. Song of Solomon 2:15–17 says, "Catch all the foxes, those little foxes, before they ruin the vineyard" (NLT). I believe Solomon's warning here is a wake-up call to all of us to beware of the "little sins" that start small and are kept secret. They can destroy a whole vineyard and ruin what is meant to be full of good fruit.

For me, I know I have downplayed "little sins." I have said,

"Oh, it's just music. It doesn't affect me!" or "It's just showing a little bit of skin, but it doesn't mean anything!" Can you relate? *It's just a picture. It's just a movie. It's just a steamy romance novel. It's just a couple of drinks. It's just second base with my boyfriend, not sex* . . . Today's culture likes to downplay and dilute sin, even normalizing and celebrating it. Even now, if there is a modest sex scene in a movie and only a few cuss words, I might think it was a wholesome movie, because we have been brainwashed to believe sin isn't harmful, that it's normal.

I repent often of my own desensitization toward sin. Because to know God and fear God is to hate evil, according to Scripture. Sin is evil, and there is no "small sin." My challenge to you is to catch the little foxes and deal with the few weeds before they ruin your whole vineyard—your life.

When I think of how a supposedly little thing can grow into a big problem, I think of my first time going to Disney World, when I ended up in the emergency room. That was not on the agenda, I can assure you.

I was six years old when my parents surprised me with the Disney trip as a birthday present. This was every kid's dream! I couldn't have been more excited. The rides, the food, the time with my parents . . . I couldn't wait. We decided to check in to the hotel first before making our way to the Disney park. When we got to the hotel, I saw a playground outside. I told my mom I wanted to play. She said I could play for ten minutes but to be careful. I slid off my shoes and took off running. The playground entrance had a long wooden boardwalk. As my little bare feet were moving faster than I could keep up, I tripped over a protruding piece of wood. I started crying when I noticed my knee bleeding, so my mom rushed over to help me.

When I started walking, I realized the cut knee was the least of my problems. I had a huge splinter stuck in the bottom of my foot. The splinter was so deep that my mom couldn't pull it out even with tweezers. It was getting more painful by the second, and my parents worried it would get infected if it wasn't removed quickly. So we immediately headed to the ER to get the splinter removed. I cried all the way there, thinking about them having to cut into my foot. I gave my mom a full presentation on how this little stick in my foot could just become a part of me and that there was no need to get it out. She laughed and said I should become a lawyer someday.

When we got to the hospital, I was dreading the procedure. My dad, cool and collected, reassured me that I would be okay. I wanted to believe him, but all I could think about was a large needle. The doctor tried to distract me by asking me questions, which, honestly, worked. The procedure was so fast, I barely felt it. Afterward, I got a treat, and we were off to Disney World.

My mom reminded me of that story the other day. I laughed, remembering how I was resolved to live with that splinter because I was afraid of the one moment of pain to cut it out. I'm so glad I didn't have to endure that discomfort for the rest of my life due to an unwillingness to face a temporary pain.

Some of us have sin splinters. We're living with sin in our lives, tolerating it, limping around with it, afraid to confront it because of the pain it might bring or the trouble we would have to go through to cut it out. But the longer that sin splinter stays in, the more it hinders our peace, purpose, and identity.

Don't kid yourself into thinking sin will go away on its own. That splinter in my foot would have gotten infected, possibly infecting my entire body. Not to be dramatic, but infections can lead to death. Similarly, unattended sin spreads quickly, and if we don't cut it out and deal with it, it will spread and infect everything.

THE SIN SLAYER

When I was praying through what to title this book, my mentor Jennie Allen, bestselling author and a rockstar of a human being, suggested I call it *Sin Slayer.* We laughed and decided that probably wasn't the best title for this book, but I thought it was too funny to leave it out of the book completely. In this chapter, we have talked about the seriousness of sin, and that Satan lures us into sin with pretty things. But there is a greater power at play here—the One who overcame and defeated sin. In Jennie's words, He is "the One who slays sin." In Him we are set free from sin. The waves of sin that used to take us out are now waves of His grace that set us free.

Jesus saw all your sin—past, present, and future—and He still chose the cross. He still said, "You are worth it. I'll take your place." He took on our sin and shame so that we could have life. He set us free from sin by *becoming* sin and paying the price none of us could . . . with His life. And He defeated sin by rising from the grave three days later.

The truth is that only the Son can set us free from the stronghold of sin. We cannot save ourselves, nor can we be saved by a fellow sinner. It takes someone perfect to save someone imperfect. The liberator from our bondage has to come from outside of enslaved humanity—and He already has. We truly walk free when we focus on our Savior instead of our sin.

> We truly walk free when we focus on our
> Savior instead of our sin.

One of my favorite stories in the Bible is in John 8, where Jesus encounters a woman caught in the act of adultery. Many surrounded her, ready to stone her for her sin. But Jesus stopped them, bent down to the woman's level, lifted up her head, and called her daughter. He bestowed an identity on her, reminding her that she didn't have to be defined by sin any longer. He didn't speak to whom she had been; He spoke to whom she could be. But he didn't just show her grace. He gave her truth, calling her out of her sin not to humiliate her but to help her.

By acknowledging her sin, then instructing her to repent and stop sinning, Jesus gave her hope that her life could go on in freedom. In the same way, whatever sin you may be stuck in or struggling with, Jesus meets you there, but He loves you too much to leave you that way. He calls you out of sin because He made you for freedom.

So, if I am really saved, will I never sin again? Unfortunately, you will sin again, and so will I. We live in a sinful, fallen world. However, there is a difference between falling into sin and living in sin. When we as believers fall into sin and then immediately confess and repent, turning from our sin and turning to God, we are forgiven and can walk in the light and truth. But for those who use God's grace as an excuse to continue to follow their own sinful cravings and pleasures, there is no true relationship with Jesus.

The only way to live free from sin is to cut off any sin and all temptation triggers. Just as the splinter required intentional removal, so does your sin. It will not naturally go away on its own. Jesus speaks about this intentional cutting off of sin in Matthew 5:29–30: "If your right eye causes you to stumble, gouge it out and throw it away. It is better for you to lose one part of your body than for your whole body to be thrown into hell. And if your right hand causes you to stumble, cut it off and throw it away. It is better for you to lose one part of your body than for your whole body to go into hell."

Jesus said to cut it off. The first step to being victorious in defeating sin is to identify what the "right hand" is in your life. It may be social media, sexting, a relationship, Xbox, steamy romance movies or novels, or online sites that are feeding your cravings. It may be alcohol, drugs, sex, lying, cheating, gossiping, or something else. Whatever it is, cut it off.

Although sin can feel stronger than us and can make us think that we have no other option, we are reminded in 1 Corinthians 10:13, "No temptation has overtaken you except what is common to mankind. And God is faithful; he will not let you be tempted beyond what you can bear. But when you are tempted, he will also provide a way out so that you can endure it." Which means we will never, ever be in a position where we *have* to sin. There will always be an option to choose holiness, righteousness, and godliness. For those of us who are believers, the Spirit that is in us is greater than the sin that is at work around and against us.

Sin brings heaviness and darkness. But God wants us to live in joy and light. Only by breaking free from sin can we find hope, happiness, and the purpose He created us for. In the same way that the lifeguard was pleading with us to stay out of the dangerous and dark waters, so our Jesus pleads with us to stay away from the dangers and darkness of sin—not to withhold anything from us, but to save us, heal us, and free us.

The thing about sin is that it always leads to something else: shame, which is where we are going next on our journey. Together, we'll continue to defeat Satan's lies that bind and to live out the truth that sets us free.

TRUTH FOR YOU

Sin promises delight but leads to death.
Our Savior defeated sin so that in Him we may have life.

6

TRUTH ABOUT SHAME

I used to wet the bed.

This was a struggle for me that started when I was young but continued all throughout middle school. I would go to sleep, only to wake up lying in a puddle. *Disgusting, right?* I agree, but I'm trying to be real.

One day I was invited to a friend's birthday party. I was so excited until I found out it was an overnight party. *Oh no! What if I wet the bed?* I tried not to think about it so I could just have fun with my friends, but when bedtime came and I saw that we would all be sleeping next to each other, I was full of fear.

I finally got to sleep. When I woke up early in the morning before everyone else, I noticed that, sure enough, I had wet the bed. There was a girl asleep right next to me. *This is a nightmare!* I thought to myself. I quietly got up and went to the bathroom to wash off and change clothes. I called my mom and asked her to come and pick me up early. I didn't say a word to anyone.

I was full of shame. Terrible thoughts filled my mind, like,

You're so disgusting. No one will ever want to be your friend or invite you back, and *What is wrong with you? You are too old to be wetting the bed.* I felt ashamed of something I couldn't control.

Thankfully, those friends did continue to invite me and hang out with me. And, yes, thankfully I did grow out of my bed-wetting problem. But what I have learned since then is that shame isn't tied to circumstances or age. It tries to follow us and define us all throughout our lives.

Maybe you have had a moment like mine. Or a moment much deeper than that. A moment of deep shame over an inappropriate picture you sent that got forwarded, a sexual decision you made, a time you got drunk and acted crazy. Or maybe your shame came from something that happened to you, like being called hurtful words, getting bullied, getting taken advantage of, feeling responsible for your parents' divorce, or getting cheated on. Whatever your shame moments have looked like, I am sorry for what you've been through and what has been done to you. I also want you to know there is hope for you, and there is hope that you can break free. Shame doesn't have to follow you or live in you. You can break up with it once and for all.

I also want to be clear that there is a big difference between embarrassment, guilt, shame, and conviction. We often confuse them and think they are all the same. Let me give you some personal examples so you can see what I mean.

Embarrassment was when I accidentally had my dress tucked into my bathing suit bottoms as I shopped around Target, until a nice lady told me. My face turned red. I fixed it. And then I moved on with my life.

Guilt was when, in high school, I got caught sneaking out of my house to go to a party when my parents were out of town and my grandmother was watching me. I felt terrible for what I did and for the anxiety I caused my grandmother.

Conviction was when I reacted with harsh words toward my spouse, my mom, or a friend, and then I immediately felt rebuked by the Holy Spirit. The rebuke didn't lead me to hate myself, hide myself, or blame anyone else. Rather it created a desire to repent and to ask forgiveness from those I had hurt. Conviction calls us *out* to call us *higher*—and it leaves us better. Conviction leads us *to* God, not away from Him.

> Conviction calls us *out* to call us *higher*—
> and it leaves us better. Conviction leads
> us *to* God, not away from Him.

And then there's shame. Shame makes you want to hide, blame, isolate, and run. It makes you hate yourself. It makes you feel like you are the problem and that there is something wrong with you. Shame usually comes from something you have done or something someone else has done to you. Shame doesn't focus on the action; it focuses on the person. When I wet the bed, I felt shame. I hated myself for what I did. I thought I was gross, unlovable, and stupid, and I wanted to run and hide.

> Shame doesn't focus on the action;
> it focuses on the person.

Some of us aren't even aware we carry shame. But we've all felt it. Maybe you can relate to one of these situations: You didn't get invited to a party that everyone else did. You got cheated on. You were neglected or overlooked by your parents. Your parents criticized you in front of other people. You got taken advantage of, or you were bullied for being different. Although the outward causes may look different, shame often leaves the same feelings in us all.

WHAT IS SHAME?

Shame is that intensely painful feeling that makes you feel unworthy of love and belonging. Shame will keep you up at night. I've had nights tossing and turning, losing sleep because of shame. It whispers, *"You are a screwup. You're damaged goods. You don't belong anywhere. You are the problem."* It doesn't take long for those whispers to turn into beliefs and for those beliefs to turn into our identity. And when shame becomes our identity, it creates misery.

How does shame even start? Where does it come from? It starts with Satan and his tendency to twist things. Like we talked about in chapter two, Satan's quest is to steal life, joy, and freedom through deception. He starts off offering us pleasure, but as soon as we give in to the temptation, he breaks his promise. We reap the deadly fruit of despair, deceit, and darkness.

Our pastor, Jonathan Pokluda, says that Satan switches price tags. Just like with sin, he presents something to you that looks desirable, like it won't cost you anything. Then after you fall for it, it ends up costing you more than you were willing to pay. Satan may start off as the tempter, but after we sin, he turns into the accuser. *"Look what you did!" "God could never forgive you or love you now!" "How could you call yourself a Christian?"* Shame is usually a result of sin, either ours or someone else's. And shame isolates us. It keeps us from being known and loved.

> Satan may start off as the tempter, but after we sin,
> he turns into the accuser.

But shame didn't enter the world the first time you felt bad about your sin. It started long before you were even born. It's *nearly* as old as humanity itself. Shame was not a part of the original creation. In Genesis 2, we read one of the most profound verses on shame in the entire Bible. Genesis 2:25 describes Adam and Eve in the Garden of Eden: "And the man and his wife were both naked and were not ashamed" (ESV). This verse is speaking to the physical nudity of the couple, but it's also speaking to a lot more. This verse tells us that there were no barriers at all between Adam and Eve. No shame. No hiding. Just perfect connection and blissful freedom.

The Bible could have said the man and woman were naked and really happy, because hey, who wouldn't be? Or it could have said they were naked and not afraid. There's an endless number of words that could have been. Why do you think there was such an intentional emphasis on lack of shame?

If we fast-forward in the story, Adam and Eve fell for Satan's temptation. They sinned. But they never expected what followed. The sin didn't deliver the power, goodness, and status that Eve had originally hoped for. Sin turned to shame, which led to Adam and Eve hiding and covering up, and eventually it created separation in their marriage and in their relationship with God.

Let's look at what happened in Genesis 3:7–10,

> Then the eyes of both of them were opened, and they realized they were naked; so they sewed fig leaves together *and made coverings for themselves.* Then the man and his wife heard the sound of the LORD God as he was walking in the garden in the cool of the day, and *they hid* from the LORD God among the trees of the garden. But the LORD God called to the man, "Where are you?" He answered, "I heard you in the garden, and *I was afraid* because I was naked; *so I hid.*"

Genesis shows us that from the beginning of time these have been the natural responses to feelings of shame:

1. **Avoidance:** We do not like the feeling of shame, so we do what we can to avoid it. In Genesis, Adam and Eve realized they were naked, so they covered up with fig leaves. Similarly, we avoid our shame by pushing it under the rug. Maybe we numb our feelings with substances, ignore them completely, or shut down emotionally.

2. **Isolation:** We withdraw. Adam and Eve ran away from

God and tried to hide. Today, we respond to shame by isolating and withdrawing from others, removing ourselves from the situation, locking ourselves in our rooms and refusing to respond to anyone's messages or knocks, hiding behind digital devices, or even busying our schedules.

3. **Attacking ourselves:** The shame within us tells us we are the problem and always will be. We might say or think, "I'm so stupid," "I hate myself for that!" "I should have known better," "It's all my fault."

4. **Blaming others:** *With shame, we blame.* We point the finger at others to avoid facing our own feelings of shame and self-hatred. Later in the passage, Adam shifts blame to Eve and tells God that the fault belongs to "the woman you put here with me" (verse 12). Then we see that Eve blames Satan. She says, "The serpent deceived me" (verse 13). We deflect shame by suggesting we are not at fault for the way we are. We blame everyone else rather than draw circles around ourselves. We blame our parents, the church, our spouses, our friends, siblings, co-workers, or bosses.

Shame creates a broken identity when what we have done or what has been done to us begins to shape how we view ourselves and God. Satan's goal is to isolate you and destroy your relationships with God, yourself, and others. *And the more we hide, the more power shame has.*

"I AM WHAT I'VE DONE"

Did you ever play hide-and-seek growing up? It was one of my favorite games to play with my sisters or cousins when I was young. I would always try to scout out the best hiding spot before anyone else even thought about it. I would keep mental notes in my head about the size of the cabinets, the random closets no one paid attention to, and I would even see if there was some sort of dresser I could squeeze into. I took the game very seriously.

Being the seeker was always fun—finding people and catching them in their hiding spots. I would feel like an FBI agent, thinking to myself, *They can't hide, and they can't outrun me either!* When it came to having to hide, I'll be honest, finding a hiding spot and crawling in some dark and tight space started out fun, but after a minute of not being found, I would begin to get scared. Usually, my hiding spots were so good no one could find me. I would turn myself in after a couple of minutes because of how scared I was being all alone in the dark.

As a kid I learned that hiding in dark places was lonely and scary. Now nearing thirty, I can attest that hiding is still lonely and scary. As kids we hid for fun and games. As teenagers and adults, we hide because of shame. We withdraw, isolate, and cover up because of something we have done or something that has been done to us. In shame we think to ourselves, *I am the problem. I am gross. I am damaged goods. I am too far gone. I am dirty. I am ugly. I am stupid.* Notice how each one starts with the "I am" statement. Shame doesn't focus on the action of what's been done; it focuses on the identity of the person.

As kids we hid for fun and games. As teenagers
and adults, we hide because of shame.

A big part of my story that I will share throughout this
book is my past struggle with pornography. Lust was a big
temptation for me from a young age, whether that was being
boy crazy and fantasizing, feeling tempted in a relationship
to push boundaries, or looking at things online when no one
was around. When I gave in to that temptation, I would feel
fine for a while, then later a shame-like heartburn would kick
in. In the quiet and the dark of night, I'd berate myself and
question my purpose. I'd be filled with frustration, self-hatred,
and angry thoughts. I'd feel distanced from God, insecure,
lonely, and I'd think, *Madi, how could you do this and call yourself
a Christian? What would your parents think of you? Girls don't struggle
with this. You better not let anyone ever find out or they will think you are
disgusting!*

Shame didn't just make me feel bad over what I had done.
Shame made me feel bad about who I was. And the longer I
kept it in the dark, the longer I sat amid those toxic and shame-
ful thoughts. I've learned that shame spreads in secrecy and
thrives in isolation.

One of the enemy's most dangerous schemes is to trap us
in what we've done or what has happened to us. He whispers
shaming lies like, *"You are what you have done," "You are too far
gone," "No one would ever want you now"*—and the list goes on. He
blurs the lines between the action of what was done and the
person who did it. And a lot of the time we believe him. We
begin to have looping negative and toxic thoughts about our-

selves. We start to feel insecure. We then feel lonely and distant from God and our godly friends. This is exactly where the enemy wants us, covered in shame and separated from God and His people—bound.

Truth be told, we won't know what hope and freedom feel like until we bring those shaming lies into the light. Until we confess our sins and share our secrets, we will continue to feel bound and burdened by them.

Whatever that sin struggle is for you, whatever that temptation is, it's going to grow and multiply in secrecy and isolation. Secrets make you sick. Secrets weigh you down. Hiding them may feel like your only option. I know, because that's what I felt. But let me tell you what else I know: You feel burdened. You feel isolated. It is dark and heavy, and it feels like the shadow of death. Because the enemy not only wants you to believe the lie that "You are what you have done," he also wants you to experience that lie all alone. But just like in my childhood game of hide-and-seek, where I would get scared of secret, lonely places, we feel safe when we stop hiding. We weren't meant for darkness.

Secrets make you sick.

Hiding isn't our answer. What we keep in the dark gains power. That's where Satan gets a foothold—in secrecy. He leads us into temptation to sin, and then sin leads to shame. Then shame creates separation, which makes us vulnerable to more sin. It's a pattern. A cycle.

Satan's lies → Sin → Shame → Separation from God and godly people.

And it's a cycle that keeps repeating—until we break it.

IT'S TIME TO BREAK UP

Have you ever been in a bad relationship? If so, it is likely that you heard from those around you that love you, "I think it's time to break up." Shame is like a bad relationship—one of those toxic ones that you try to kick to the curb, but somehow it keeps bouncing back. Because even though you may break up with shame, shame doesn't usually break up with you. Whether it is something you've done that you regret or something that is completely out of your control, shame always tries to come crawling back. But there are ways to fight. I've already shared one of those ways—confession. To kill shame is to confess shame. When we bring what is dark into the light, it becomes light.

To kill shame is to confess shame.

The enemy wants to keep you bound by shame and hold you captive in your regrets, insecurities, and fears. But God wants to set you free and give you light and life again. He promises that when we confess to Him with a repentant heart, He forgives us. And when we confess to others, we experience healing.

Shame is not who you are. You are not your mistakes—no matter how large or small. You are not damaged goods. You are not too far gone. Your past does not define you. In Christ, we are new creations. You don't have to be defined by your broken yesterdays. Your past can stay your past. You can walk into your beautiful tomorrows with Jesus in the light. You don't have to let your past define you. So, if you have regrets about your past or are currently carrying shame, my prayer for you is Romans 8:1, where the Word of God reminds us "there is now no condemnation for those of us who are in Christ Jesus." In Christ we are washed white as snow.

Have I done things I deeply regret? Yes! Have I been extremely hurt by others? Yes! Have I had moments of feeling ashamed of who I am? Yes. But as I've allowed the Lord to redefine me, I've realized that I am loved, free, and redeemed. He uses the mess of my yesterdays for the message of His goodness for today and tomorrow.

If you feel defined by your sin and past mistakes, you're not alone. Usually, the enemy's accusations have less to do with who you *have been* and more to do with who you *could be*. That idea terrifies him. So, when he starts reminding you of your past, you start reminding him of his future—because yours is eternal light and life, and his is eternal darkness and torment.

And the best news of all time? Jesus defeated shame. He hung on the cross, stripped naked, and took on our sin and shame. He became a public display of shame on our behalf, and He died the worst death possible. He did all this so we could get back to our original state: naked and unashamed, right with God, loved and accepted and joyful.

His love rescues us from the grip of sin and shame. He came to deliver us from things that we thought we'd never be free from. He comes to cleanse us from our dirty mess and give us a new and everlasting hope. Those things that used to bring pain can bring joy and can be used for a purpose. It's not about what you have done; it's about what Jesus chose to do for you.

> It's not about what you have done;
> it's about what Jesus chose to do for you.

We can walk in hope and freedom not because we're strong or have such willpower or virtue. It's not by our efforts, but by the finished work of Jesus Christ on the cross. He died and rose again in three days, defeating Satan, sin, and shame.

Here's a truth that I want you to hear: Shame can stop us from drawing near to God, but it does not stop God from drawing near to us. Picking back up with the story in Genesis 3, when Adam and Eve were hiding from God after they sinned against Him, God began searching for them. God is not ashamed of you and what you've done. He doesn't abandon you after you have sinned and fallen short. He doesn't want to see you stuck in sin or hiding in shame. He wants to see you free and thriving! And He knows the only way that happens is if you come out of hiding and run to Him. He loves you and He searches for you, not to judge you and hurt you, but to heal you and free you!

> Shame can stop us from drawing near to God, but it
> does not stop God from drawing near to us.

God deals with our shame by shining the spotlight. Because when shame is brought into the light, it loses its power. His first question when Adam and Eve hid from Him was, "Where are you?" God already knew, but He was lovingly getting Adam to acknowledge his position. God wanted Adam to confess—not to humiliate him, but to heal him.

For me, breaking free from shame required me to confess sin and other embarrassing struggles out loud—whether I felt ashamed of my bed-wetting problem, or a much deeper shame that taunted me. The lies I had internalized didn't dwindle immediately, nor did the temptation to sin, but as I continued to rely on the Holy Spirit and live in the light with community and accountability, it became easier and easier to resist temptation and to pursue holiness with all my heart.

Where shame ends, grace begins. Shame tells us that our death sentence is that we will never be enough and that we are stuck in our sin. Grace meets us at the door of our insecurities and pain and invites us to be free. Grace agrees that we are weak and sinful, but it leads us to the Truth and the Truth sets us free. It's time to break up with shame, because God has broken shame for you.

If you're feeling shame today, know that God hasn't given up on you. So don't give up on Him. There's no need to waste guilt on yesterday or worry on tomorrow. The Bible reminds us that worldly sorrow is what leads to shame, but godly sorrow is what leads us to repentance. Not only does God want you and me to experience freedom from bondage here on this earth, but more than anything He wants us to experience life with Him forever, in eternity.

TRUTH FOR YOU

The enemy wants to define you by your scars.

Jesus already defined you by His scars.

7

TRUTH ABOUT ETERNITY

Let me start at the beginning. It was a crazy day. I was at a friend's bachelorette party on an island. That may sound like a wild time. It wasn't. Truly, we ate and laid out on the beach the whole time. It was wonderful. But the one thing about this island is that it was not easy to get to.

I was the only one of our group who had to leave early so I could make it to another close friend's wedding. I packed my bags and rode a golf cart over to the water trolley at 5 A.M. Once the boat started moving, I didn't feel well. I got seasick, and I had to make a beeline to the onboard bathroom. Puking, I knew I eventually was going to have to go back out with everyone else where they would see my pale skin, shaky hands, and vomit hair. Disgusting, right? But I couldn't stay in the bathroom forever.

The boat ride was about two hours, and I was trying to do everything to keep from vomiting and running back to the bathroom again. Thankfully, I held it together and we arrived safely on shore. All of this happened before 7 A.M. What a start to the day! I now had to Uber two hours to the closest airport. Once I got to the airport and made it to my gate, the airline attendant announced the flight would be delayed. I decided it would be a good time for me to clean myself up. Although I didn't have any spare clothes, I washed my face with water and wiped off a few stains on my clothes. When I got back to the gate to wait on this delayed flight, I thought to myself, *Okay, let's open the Bible. I really need Jesus today!*

Hours later, we boarded our flight, and I began working on my second book manuscript, *The Love Everybody Wants*, during this three-hour flight. My book-writing process is to type out the manuscript on my computer, then print the whole thing for read-throughs, edits, and finalizing the flow. So I whipped out my massive 250-page stack of papers, confusing the poor man next to me, and started editing. I went through half of the manuscript and was feeling good about my productivity. Three hours later, we arrived.

Because of the flight delay, I wasn't sure if I would make my connecting flight. When I rushed to my gate for the flight, it had already closed. I begged the gate attendant to let me on, explaining the flight delay situation and that I had a wedding rehearsal to be at, fully dressed by 6 P.M. (It was 4 P.M. and I was still in my vomit-covered clothes.) She apologized and told me my only option was to get my bags at baggage claim, go back to ticketing, and try to get on a new flight.

When I arrived at ticketing, they informed me that the only other flight was going out in twenty minutes, and it was past baggage check-in and the flight was full. I pleaded with her. I begged. I offered money. I asked for other solutions. I asked about other flights, but there were none until the next day. I even had my mother-in-law call and talk to the lady. (Moms fix everything, right?)

It was no use. She told me my only option was to find a hotel nearby or stay at the airport and check back early the next morning—the day of the wedding! I was stressed but knew I had no other option. I found a hotel nearby and paid way too much for a room, but at that point I didn't care. I got in my room and went to grab my book manuscript to work a bit more—and noticed it was gone. All 250 pages. Gone. It hit me in that moment—I left it on the plane. At this point I wanted to scream and cry. But instead, I ordered a pepperoni pizza, took a bath, and went to bed at 8 P.M. Thankfully, the next day was much better. I did in fact make my flight this time and made it in time for the wedding.

I didn't share this story with you just to complain about my day. I share this because I think it is a picture of many of us in the world today, thinking that the universe will give us what we need and all flights will take us to the same destination. But Jesus tells us in the Bible that not everyone who thinks they have a ticket will make it on the plane. Not all tickets are the same and not all planes are headed to the same place. And some people think they can live it up now and get serious about their faith later, and will arrive at the gate to realize . . . the gate has been closed.

I want to make sure you have a true ticket. And that you make it to the right destination.

Jesus says in Matthew 7:13–14, "Enter through the narrow

gate. For wide is the gate and broad is the road that leads to destruction, and many enter through it. But small is the gate and narrow the road that leads to life, and only a few find it." Jesus is saying here that not all gates lead to the right destination, and many are on the path to destruction.

This is the truth most don't want to hear or accept. We all want to believe that everyone makes it to heaven, no matter how they live their life or what they believe—they just need to be a "good person." Right? Jesus tells us plainly that is not the case. And although this is a hard and intense conversation to have, it's an important one. Because the Bible is clear—many will be deceived, and I don't want that to be you or me.

Jesus says that the belief that all roads lead to life and heaven is *not* true. There is only *one* way, and He says, "It's Me." The world's teachings might seem "loving" in the moment—that it's acceptable to live however you want and do whatever you want to do. However, it's unloving in the end, because it isn't true. Convincing someone that a lie is the truth is mean. If the truth is that Jesus is the only way, and He is the One who leads to eternal life forever, why would we teach anything else? What sounds nice in the moment but leads to an eternity of darkness and torment *isn't* nice.

What if the gate lady had told me that I could just choose any flight I wanted and that all the flights would take me to where I want to go? I might really like what she was saying and think it was great news! I could have picked a plane and ended up in some random, war-torn country, trapped and unable to get home. Her telling me that any plane would take me where I want to go and that "all ways are the right way" might have sounded loving in the moment, but it would later prove not to be loving at all.

We may have a gospel of grace, but we also have a gospel of truth. What we don't have is a gospel of tolerance. Jesus did not come to tolerate sin; He came to abolish it. So I want to break your belief that just any ticket can get you where you want to go, and build your belief in the *true* ticket—Jesus as the way, the truth, and the life.

LIES ABOUT ETERNITY

Anyone else obsessed with frogs? *No? Just me?* Perfect. Well, at least I used to be. Not so much anymore. When I was little, I'd search at the tree line between the playground and the woods during recess looking for those cute little guys. I wanted to catch one and bring it home so we could be forever friends. When I finally caught one, I carefully put it in my little backpack with some grass and leaves to make it feel comfy.

The next day, when my mom went to put my lunch in my bag, a horrible smell hit her nose. Poor mom! This happened a couple of times. Finally, she said, "Madison, you cannot bring frogs home. Frogs need light, they need oxygen, they need water. They're not made to be shut up in a little girl's backpack all afternoon."

It's true. Frogs are not made for backpacks.

You and I are in a little girl's backpack right now—otherwise known as our world. Frogs weren't made for backpacks, and we were not made for this world. God made us to be with Him and to have eternal life with Him. *And until we die, we're just living in this world as foreigners with finite time.*

Ecclesiastes 3:11 says, "He has made everything beautiful in its time. He has also set eternity in the human heart; yet no one can fathom what God has done from beginning to end." Did you catch that? We're made with eternity in our hearts. That's why this world and all it has to offer can never fully satisfy.

Let's address some of the lies from Satan that keep us from knowing and believing the truth about eternity.

1. "Live it up now."

Satan has convinced our world and culture today of the YOLO principle—you only live once. Satan wants us to believe, "You're gonna die one day, so live it up now and do everything you want to do now!" This is a theme all over social media, in all the popular songs on the radio, and in Hollywood movies. It's a feel-good pep talk. *YOLO. Live your best life now. You do you!*

We have been deceived to believe the lie that money makes us feel happy, important, and secure, and that material things like fancy houses, cars, and followers will satisfy our souls. The world today promotes "live it up now" and teaches us to chase whatever brings us instant happiness and pleasure.

But just like Ecclesiastes tells us, we weren't made to be satisfied or secure in anything this world can offer us; we were made for eternity. For we brought nothing into this world, and we can take nothing out of it. There's no way to take anything with you when you die—not your body, your boyfriend, your car, or your job. That stuff is temporary. Instead of trying to get rich, get famous, or get attention and power, we are told by God to invest in an eternal kingdom, where joy never ends and treasures never fade away. A tornado or a crashing economy tomorrow could wipe out everything you have and all you have built, but an eternity in heaven is secure and everlasting.

Interestingly, I have met some of the wealthiest, most famous, and most powerful people in the world. I could drop names that would drop your jaw. And you know what I can confidently say? If they don't know Jesus, they don't know hope. They don't know joy. They don't know purpose. Most of those who don't know Jesus are depressed, anxious, hopeless, and miserable. That's because they're pouring body and soul into this worldly life, and it's just not a good investment.

In Matthew Perry's memoir, *Friends, Lovers, and the Big Terrible Thing*, which came out just ten months before his death, he said, "I am constantly filled with a lurking loneliness, a yearning, clinging to the notion that something outside of me will fix me. But I had all that the outside had to offer!"* and "You have to get famous to know that it's not the answer. And nobody who is not famous will ever truly believe that."† A man who had it "all"—fame, wealth, multiple houses, celebrity love and relationships, and sex—was depressed, addicted

* Matthew Perry, *Friends, Lovers, and the Big Terrible Thing: A Memoir* (Flatiron Books, 2022), 3.
† Matthew Perry, *Friends, Lovers, and the Big Terrible Thing*, 81.

to drugs, lonely, and constantly longing for something more. That's because he was made for more. And so were you.

In Matthew 16:26 it says, "What do you benefit if you gain the whole world but lose your own soul?" (NLT). Those who have nothing in this world and those who have everything will all face the same reality as they near death, asking the question, *What really matters?* They will also face the same reality in the next life. For we will all have to stand face-to-face with God and give an account of our lives. How we choose to spend our time here will determine where and how we will spend eternity.

> How we choose to spend our time here will determine where and how we will spend eternity.

Life on earth is all just pregame, warm-up, dress-rehearsal stuff, and how we practice here will determine if we win or lose after death. Yet the outcome of where we spend eternity is not "muster up your strength and go win the game," but rather "the game has already been won for you. You only need to pick the right team." Jesus paid the price for our ticket. However, we still have to accept that ticket and get on the right plane—the one that leads to eternal life.

2. "Because I am a good person, I will make it to heaven."

Let's say you died and went to heaven, and there Jesus asked you, "Why should I let you in?" What would you say?

A lie that many believe is that their good deeds and efforts will win them a ticket into heaven. When I have asked this question to Uber drivers, passengers on a flight next to me, waitresses, and even attendees at my speaking events at universities, most respond, "Because I went to church." Or the classic, "I was a good person." But those answers are incorrect. The answer is not "I." The answer is "He." It's not what you do or don't do that gains you eternal life. It's what He—Jesus—did for you.

> It's not what you do or don't do that gains you
> eternal life. It's what He—Jesus—did for you.

Many of us are deceived and believe the lie that our good works and religious traditions, our notable moral acts, will get us into heaven. But Jesus says in John 14:6, "I am the way and the truth and the life. No one comes to the Father except through me." Jesus makes the controversial claim that He is the only way. There are not multiple ways to heaven. And we cannot create our own way there either. It's not by our efforts or works but by His grace alone that we are saved.

There are many lies about ways we can be saved or ways we can make it to heaven, but Jesus says in John 10:9–10, "I am the gate; whoever enters through me will be saved. . . . The thief comes only to steal and kill and destroy; I have come that they may have life, and have it to the full." He addresses the fact that there is a liar who is after our eternity. If we choose to follow and believe his lies, it will lead to a path of destruction and death. But if we choose to accept the gift of Jesus and follow His truth, it will bring us life to the fullest!

The thing about Jesus is that although He is the only way to eternal life, He made a way for you to get to Him. He came to you. He doesn't ask you to clean yourself up and work hard enough to maybe, possibly make it up to Him. Unlike the lie of, "If you are good enough, you might make it into heaven . . . good luck!" Jesus says, "I'll be good enough *for* you, and through Me, you can have a sure ticket into heaven." In Him all are accepted and invited, but not all choose to accept Him.

3. "Hell is a big party and heaven is boring."

One lie that has become popular and made its way into pop culture music and media is that hell is just one big party and there will be lots of drinkin' it up and shoutin' aloud. I can't even count the number of jokes I have heard in movies, TV shows, and music alluding to the idea that everyone in hell will be drinking beer and having a good ole time. There are celebrities who have music videos dancing with the devil, dressing up as the devil, and mocking Jesus being crucified on the cross. This has become normalized in today's world.

But the truth is that hell is not a party. It is the highest form of torment, darkness, and misery one could ever experience. Revelation 14:11 says, "And the smoke of their torment goes up forever and ever, and they have no rest, day or night" (ESV). According to 2 Thessalonians 1:9, those in hell "will suffer the punishment of eternal destruction, away from the presence of the Lord and from the glory of his might" (ESV). And Jesus describes hell in Matthew 13:50 as the place "where there will be weeping and gnashing of teeth."

Clearly hell is awful. It's torment. It's not a party; rather it's complete and total separation from God. There is no goodness there, no hope, and no second chance. Hell is not a party I'd want to go to.

Not only do a lot of people view hell as one big party, but many view heaven as a boring and miserable place to be. The lie is that in heaven we are just going to be a bunch of angels, floating around with wings with nothing to do. The idea of heaven for many people brings anxiety and confusion.

But the truth about eternity in heaven is found in Revelation 21:4–5:

> " 'He will wipe every tear from their eyes. There will be no more death' or mourning or crying or pain, for the old order of things has passed away." He who was seated on the throne said, "I am making everything new!"

No more crying? No more pain? No more death? Can you even imagine a life of no worry, anxiety, relational tension and stress, rejection, depression, or death? Jesus described heaven in Luke 23:43 as "paradise."

Heaven is the *real* and *true* party—where there is no shame, sadness, sickness, or Satan! *How amazing does that sound?*

The truth about eternity is that it's where you pay for your life on earth. One option is eternal happiness in heaven, and one is eternal torment in hell. In heaven, your sins are paid for and conquered by Jesus. In hell, *you* pay for your sins forever. Hell is eternal punishment—not a punishment that is cruel and unlawful, but one that is just. For we serve a just God.

The enemy deceives the world with mantras and beliefs like *YOLO, carpe diem, heaven isn't real, hell is just a big party*. Going along with this way of thinking may seem harmless, but it's a trap that leads to bondage and death, not freedom and life. The good news is that Jesus—the Truth with a capital *T*— died to set us free from the lies of Satan, the grip of sin, and the tyranny of the world. He conquered death and made a clear path for us into eternity. Eternity is secure for those of us who know the Truth.

Y.O.L.T

One day when I was on a flight, I felt an urge to share the gospel with the guy next to me. But he seemed like the kind of guy that relied on logic, reason, and science—I could tell by the five-hundred-page physics and philosophy book he was reading. I had a lot of work to do, so I tried to just ignore that feeling. But the Holy Spirit tugged on my heart again. So I took out my earbuds and turned to him, tapped him on the shoulder, and said, "Can I ask you a question?" *I guess I am in it now,* I thought. I asked, "What is truth to you?"

Why that was my first question I have no idea. He went on to talk for another thirty minutes about the earth, its formation, how humans played a role in it all, and how the Universe will bless and reward those who are good to it.

I went on to ask him about his personal story. Then I asked him what he thought about religion and God. He informed me that religion isn't necessary but is rather an option and outlet for people to express themselves. He said, "I don't need God for inward peace."

Then I asked him, "If you died today, what do you think happens? Where will you be?" Sort of an eerie question to ask someone as they are flying on the same plane you are on, sitting right next to you. I prayed in my mind, *Lord, please don't let us die. I just want him to know You.*

He went on to say that because he has been a good person, he believed he would make it to heaven. We talked the rest of the hour-and-a-half plane ride, and I shared with him the full gospel: that because of the death and resurrection of Jesus, we can be saved, free from sin and shame, with full assurance that we will go to heaven. I told him that our salvation, our ticket to eternal life, wasn't based on our own efforts or good deeds, but rather on the free gift Jesus offers us. I could see the wheels in his mind turning. As we started to land, I was bummed that the conversation didn't end with him accepting Jesus into his heart. But I have prayed for him since that moment and hope that, if not now, one day he will choose to follow Jesus.

When I reflected on that conversation, it made me think about how the enemy has deceived many into believing they are the ticket to their own salvation. The enemy has also led others to believe that they should live life up and do whatever they want since "you only live once."

I pray that if you are on the fence or have believed those lies up until this point, the Holy Spirit would reveal to you the truth—the truth about your life here and the truth about eternity. Because "YOLO" is a lie, but the truth is "YOLT"—you only live twice. And how you live here will determine how and where you live next.

Remember that song by Coldplay called "Paradise"? I can hear it playing in my head even as I type this chapter: "This could be PARA-PARA-PARADISE!" Paradise is what Jesus promises for those who love and follow Him. And not the kind of paradise that gets ruined by a cloudy or rainy day. The kind of paradise that goes on forever and ever, in perfect, eternal bliss and joy. Psalm 16:11 says, "In your presence is fullness of joy; at your right hand are pleasures forevermore" (NKJV).

Everything we were made for and everything we long for is found in Jesus. And because of Jesus, we can have full confidence on where we will spend eternity. For He is the true ticket, the Truth that leads to life—life forevermore!

TRUTH FOR YOU

How you choose to spend your life on earth will determine where and how you will spend your life in eternity.

8

DARE TO BE TRUE

Have you ever played truth or dare?

I played it one time my sophomore year of high school, and it didn't end well. I ended up having to do things I wouldn't normally do. Being daring in that game meant I had to prank people, compromise values, and even risk my own life. I walked away from that experience saying, "Never again!"

But I want us to play, or rather live out, truth *and* dare— a challenge that will not lead to regret or shame, but rather joy and freedom. The first half of this book we focused on truth. We confronted lies that bind us and keep us stuck in the same sin cycles and ungodly life patterns. And we talked about the Truth that sets us free from all the lies, labels, and limitations.

Now it's time to dare. Don't be scared. This is a daring that leads you closer to Jesus, to your purpose, and ultimately to a life of freedom and peace. Instead of focusing on combatting lies with truth, from now on we will tackle the practical ways of living that truth out: how we can confront the obstacles that often keep us from living a life of abundance. How we can overcome all that holds us back.

Maybe for you, hearing and knowing the truth is the hardest part. Or maybe following the truth and daring to live it is harder. Wherever you are at this point in your journey, God has more for you. And this daring adventure is one full of hope, purpose, and life!

Remember the story I shared at the beginning of the book about my husband and me having a potentially deadly experience with our gas leak, and how we were living with something that was slowly killing us? Think how crazy it would have been if we discovered the gas leak but then decided not to take action to fix it.

In the same way, it's not enough for you to identify the lies that have been keeping you bound, sucking the life out of you, and keeping you from living out God's best. It's not enough to have an *understanding* of the truth that can break you free. We can't just identify the problem; we must fix it.

I wouldn't be here today if I'd said to the plumber, "Oh, thanks for telling me the truth about those toxic fumes. I just needed to know the issue. You can go now. Thanks." No way! With that gas leaking, we would have gotten sicker and sicker and eventually it would have taken our lives.

The truth necessitated a change. And now it's time for the truth to create change in your life.

D.T.R

But first we need to have a little D.T.R. If you don't speak acronym, I'm saying it's time to "define the relationship." Don't worry, I'm not trying to get up in your personal business. I'm talking about your relationship with Jesus.

Every relationship reaches a point where you have to define what it is and where it's going. Have you ever liked someone but lacked clarity on what the relationship status or title was, and you wondered, *What are we? Where is this going?* It can be a pretty awkward conversation. But to get to where you want to be, you have to know where you are.

So, what is your relationship like with Jesus right now? Is your relationship exclusive? Are you committed? Is it based off convictions or convenience? Is it out of duty or delight? Is it a relationship or religion? What exactly is your relationship, if you have one?

The only way to achieve true change is to be honest. You are only going to be as healthy and free as you are honest. So where are you with Jesus right now? If you had to rate your relationship—with one being *I don't have a relationship with Jesus at all,* five being *I'm unsure where I stand,* and ten being *I'm confident and secure in my personal relationship with Jesus*—what would you say? In order for our relationship with Jesus to be true, we have to be honest about where we are at currently.

You are only going to be as healthy and free as you are honest.

There was a time in my life I would've answered that question with a seven. Maybe an eight on a good day. If I prayed enough, went to church, and opened my Bible that day the number would be higher. But if I fell into sexual sin or lied or gossiped, I would rate myself a lower number. It wasn't until I went all in with Jesus—and truly understood what it meant to be saved and set free by His grace alone—that I realized that answering that question with a one through nine is all the same. In traveling all over the country and experiencing revival on college campuses, I have seen most answer that question the same way, between one and nine, most falling in the six to eight range. But the truth is that Jesus didn't die for 60 percent of your sins—or 70 percent. He either died for all your sins or none of your sins. And if you choose to follow Him and be in relationship with Him, His blood is sufficient and covers the full 100 percent of your sins—past, present, and future. So there really can only be a zero or a ten. And wherever you find yourself right now, my hope is that by the end of this chapter or book, you commit your life to Jesus and confidently answer that same question, "Ten!" And though believing in Him and receiving His grace is free, following Him will cost you something.

The reality is that a lot of us like the idea of loving Jesus but not the idea of following Him. We like His love and His blessings, but we don't really want to obey and give it all up for Him. We love Him when it's convenient, when we need something, or out of obligation. A lot of people have had goosebump moments, as tears stream down their faces, where they raise their hands or recite a prayer to accept Jesus into their hearts, but often it stops there—believing in Jesus without ever making the commitment to follow Him. What I want you to know is that to be a true Christian, the two have to be connected.

Matthew 10:37–39 says, "Anyone who loves their father or mother more than me is not worthy of me; anyone who loves their son or daughter more than me is not worthy of me. Whoever does not take up their cross and follow me is not worthy of me. Whoever finds their life will lose it, and whoever loses their life for my sake will find it." That doesn't feel like an "I raised my hand for salvation, so I'm good" kind of calling. It sounds to me like Jesus is saying, "I am your everything or I am nothing. Following Me will cost you something, yet you will gain everything you were made for." More than just an emotional moment, it's a transformational encounter that changes everything about you—how you dress, how you talk, how you love, and how you live.

I also want to point out that His invitations are addressed to *anyone*. He doesn't leave out or exclude anyone. He invites us all. The person with a sexual past? *Invited.* The person who gets drunk and high? *Invited.* The one who has been cutting himself? *Invited.* The judgmental hypocrite? *Invited.* The one who has been starving herself and hates what she sees when she looks in the mirror? *Invited.* The one who had the abortion? *Invited.* The one with suicidal thoughts? *Invited.* "Anyone" means me. "Anyone" means you. It's the greatest invitation of all time, but it's up to us to receive it and then follow.

I often think about my relationship with Jesus like my relationship with my spouse. Think how weird it would have been on the wedding to say "I do," put the rings on our fingers, do the whole ceremony and honeymoon thing, but then come back from it all only to go right back to the single life we had before—living in separate houses, maintaining individual lives, and flirting or entertaining other potential mates. That would be crazy!

Just like when you get married and say "I do," with Jesus, we have an exclusive relationship. In marriage, you make a commitment to fulfill a role. You don't walk down the aisle begrudgingly. You don't say the words "I do" resentfully or unwillingly (at least I hope not!). No, you walk down the aisle with excitement for your new covenant. You say the words "I do" with joy and eagerness to your new lifelong partner. In the same way, we follow Jesus and become one with Him, not out of a "have to" but a "get to."

When you say "I do" to Jesus and receive His Spirit, everything changes. The old you, old patterns, and old ways of living begin to die off. The new you arrives. You don't go back to living like you were before. And that type of commitment changes not only your name and your identity, but also your living situation, finances, relationships with others, and more. Following Jesus changes *everything*! To say yes to Jesus is the best yes you will ever give. It's the best yes *I* have ever given.

In order for you and me to dare to live true and free, we have to define our relationship with Jesus and ask ourselves, *Am I a true follower? Is my relationship with Jesus where it needs to be and where I want it to be? Am I following Jesus out of delight? Am I committed? Am I connected?*

DARING DIFFICULTIES

Following Jesus is the best decision you will ever make, but it doesn't mean it won't come without opposition, temptation, or resistance. There will be obstacles we will have to overcome to stay true.

Let's talk about what some of those difficulties with a daring lifestyle might be.

1. Sin

Have you ever tried to run with weights? Personally, I have not because that sounds miserable. But I know some people train like this. And what is the point of it? The weights provide resistance and slow you down. They keep you from running free and fast. Now, if we are talking about strength training, the weights are probably good because they build muscle and endurance. But the weights I want to talk about aren't the good kind. They are the kind that keep you from running your race.

Hebrews 12:1 says, "Therefore, since we are surrounded by such a great cloud of witnesses, let us throw off everything that hinders and the sin that so easily entangles. And let us run with perseverance the race marked out for us." This verse tells us that we cannot run our race for God when we are weighed down by sin. Sin keeps so many of us from abiding in Christ and bearing fruit. Sin separates us from God. We cannot live in sin and live in God at the same time.

This verse insinuates that we have to physically throw sin off. Continuously. Which means it takes intensity and intentionality. Sin is intense with us, so we have to be intense back. I am not going to spend a lot of time on this topic because we already addressed it in detail in chapter five. But it is important to acknowledge that to dare to be true and live the life God has for you, you must intentionally throw off everything that hinders you from running. Throw it off with force and don't look back! You will notice that you feel lighter. You feel freer. You feel more equipped to run.

2. Spiritual Warfare

You have a very real enemy. And that enemy is after your intimacy. That enemy is after your destiny. Therefore, spiritual warfare is real.

I remember being in a shopping mall when I heard what sounded like gunfire. Everyone panicked. What did I do? I ran as fast as I could. I later found out on the news that there was no real shooter, but I was not sticking around in that mall to figure that out. I got out of there! For most people, when they realize they are in a spiritual war they respond one of two ways: fight or flight. Most people, like me in that mall, flee as fast as possible, thinking, *I don't want to mess with Satan. If I keep my distance maybe he won't mess with me.*

But the truth is, we can't just run away from spiritual warfare and the enemy's attacks, thinking that if we run we will be safe. That's like if we got dropped off in the middle of a war zone and were told, "Don't worry. If you just pretend the missiles aren't real and the enemy isn't after you, maybe they will just go away." The enemy, Satan, is after you, and it doesn't benefit you to flee or pretend he isn't there and act like there isn't an all-out war over your soul happening.

The only way you overcome spiritual warfare is if you fight. And the weapons you are given are proven to be victorious. That's the good news. Second Corinthians 10:4–5 says, "The weapons we fight with are not the weapons of the world. On the contrary, they have divine power to demolish strongholds. We demolish arguments and every pretension that sets itself up against the knowledge of God, and we take captive every thought to make it obedient to Christ."

Not only do we have the winning weapons, we also are given a battle plan so we can be prepared to know how to win. Spiritual attack turns into spiritual authority. Ephesians 6:11–17 paints a picture of how we can combat spiritual warfare with a battle plan:

> Put on the full armor of God, so that you can take your stand against the devil's schemes. For our struggle is not against flesh and blood, but against the rulers, against the authorities, against the powers of this dark world and against the spiritual forces of evil in the heavenly realms. Therefore put on the full armor of God, so that when the day of evil comes, you may be able to stand your ground, and after you have done everything, to stand. Stand firm then, with the belt of truth buckled around your waist, with the breastplate of righteousness in place, and with your feet fitted with the readiness that comes from the gospel of peace. In addition to all this, take up the shield of faith, with which you can extinguish all the flaming arrows

of the evil one. Take the helmet of salvation and the sword
of the Spirit, which is the word of God.

In this passage we are told how to prepare for battle.
Though each of the weapons is described as physical armor,
they represent the spiritual authority God gives us. Without
Him, we are defeated. With Him, nothing can defeat us—no
devil in hell, darkness on earth, or demonic attack. We are
covered and protected in Christ.

Let's look more closely at the armor:

- the belt of truth: Who is our truth? *Jesus Christ*
- the breastplate of righteousness: Who is our righteousness? *Jesus Christ*
- the shield of faith: Who is the author and finisher of
  our faith? *Jesus Christ*
- the helmet of salvation: Who is our salvation? *Jesus
  Christ*
- the sword of the Spirit: Who is our sword (meaning the
  Word)? *Jesus Christ*
- the shoes of peace: Who is the Prince of Peace? *Jesus
  Christ*

Remember, we don't fight *for* victory, we fight *from a place* of
victory. Jesus Christ has already won. On our own, we cannot
defeat the enemy and his attacks. But with the help of Jesus
and His armor, we can advance against any troop and defeat
all enemies! There is no reason to fear the warfare when we
have the mighty Warrior on our side.

> There is no reason to fear the warfare when we have
> the mighty Warrior on our side.

3. Spiritual Immaturity

What often keeps us from being true followers of Christ is a lack of intentionality in connecting with God and others. I call this a lack of spiritual maturity. Remember how we addressed earlier in this chapter that some accept God's gift of salvation and then consider it done? They go about their lives just as before, with no real heart or life change. Where there is no life change, there is no real relationship.

> Where there is no life change,
> there is no real relationship.

The one who has been truly transformed by the love and grace of Jesus Christ longs to be with Him and desires to obey and honor Him with their life. John 15:5 talks about how we must intentionally stay connected to Him. It says, "I am the vine; you are the branches. If you remain in me and I in you, you will bear much fruit; apart from me you can do nothing." True followers of Jesus abide in Him through spiritual disciplines, such as continuously praying, plugging into a local church, serving, tithing, giving, finding accountability and godly community, reading the Word of God daily, and spending time in His presence with thanksgiving and praise. Spiritual disciplines alone don't save you, and people can do all these and still not really know Jesus intimately if they act out of the wrong heart.

Although these disciplines don't constitute the life of the believer, they do show the fruit of the believer. They cultivate dependence on God, facilitate connection, and keep you living in the light. Personally, I can't rely solely on myself or my feelings, so I know I need community, accountability, and a local church. And the longer I have walked with Jesus, the more I have learned that when I prioritize seeking Him above all, everything else falls into place. Making Him my top priority brings me abundant life.

4. Selfish "Faith"

Many people's relationships with Jesus won't stand the test of time because those relationships are about them and not about Him. They only serve or follow God when it is convenient for them or when things go according to their plan.

> Many people's relationships with Jesus won't stand the test of time because those relationships are about them and not about Him.

Some people live a double life and demand a full-time God while they have a part-time faith. They compartmentalize God into their "faith bubble," but then wonder why God isn't showing up and moving in their job bubble, spouse bubble, friendship bubble, or health bubble.

If you want a full-time God, it requires full-time faith. Your secular world shouldn't be different from your sacred world. In other words, your everyday life shouldn't look different from your spiritual life. He is your everything or He is nothing. He is the Lord of your life or something else is. The truth is that God wants every part of your life, not just some part of it.

Sometimes people become Christians and expect life to get magically easier and perfect. Like God owes them. Like God is a genie in a bottle just here to grant their wishes. Some pastors and churches preach a prosperity gospel—a belief that if you follow God, you'll be blessed. Part of that is true because God Himself is a blessing. But it doesn't mean everything in your life will *feel* blessed or that obedience always leads to material blessings.

You are not guaranteed the raise, the car, the spouse, or the social media following just because you follow God. It's not a performance- or metrics-based system. It doesn't mean if you follow God, He will give you all these worldly things and grant you all the desires of your heart. To follow Jesus is to make *Him* the desire of your heart. And to accept His great invitation is to "die" to self and to the desires and pleasures of this world in order to be made alive in Christ.

Kyle Idleman puts it this way, "[Most Christians] are by nature comfort seekers, not cross bearers."* And the reality is that most just want the crown but not the cross.

---

* Kyle Idleman, *Not a Fan* (Zondervan, 2016), 163.

DARE TO DO!

The other day as I sat down in a chair, the chair completely collapsed. After my heart stopped racing and the redness of my face disappeared, I tried to assess the problem. I then noticed that one of the legs of the chair was missing and another one was broken. No wonder I fell. I thought, *What use is this chair?* The chair couldn't operate in the way it was meant to because it didn't have strong and secure legs.

Just like that chair, your faith isn't complete or fully operating in the way it was meant to without legs. Faith has legs. Here's what I mean: You will follow what you believe in. You will share what has impacted you. Think about it: When someone finds a product or a yummy recipe or a solution to something, they share it. On the contrary, think about if you got into a relationship but you never talked about the person or posted about the person, if no one in your life met the person, and you never fully committed to being with the person. Many people would question if the relationship was real or if it was important to you. Similarly, if we call ourselves Christians but our lives don't reflect Christ in any way—we don't ever talk about Him, we don't share our faith with others, our lifestyle remains unchanged, and there is no sign of real commitment or transformation—I would question if the relationship is real.

A real faith isn't idle, contained, comfortable, or self-focused. A person who has been changed by the grace and goodness of Jesus Christ can't help but talk about it and pay it forward. Their life reflects the truth they've received. As Peter boldly proclaimed in Acts 4:20, "As for us, we cannot help speaking about what we have seen and heard." It's not enough just to say we believe in Jesus if it doesn't change our life or the lives of those around us. It's belief plus action that equals real faith. James, in the Bible, says faith without action is dead. He cuts right to the chase.

And let me be clear so it doesn't sound like I am contradicting myself. In the last chapter, I talked about how it's not our good works that save us, but the sacrifice of Jesus Christ. It's true: Your good works can't save you. But when you are saved, you *do good works*. Does that make sense? You are not saved by what you do. But if you are truly saved, you do good works in the name of Jesus. This isn't works-based salvation, but rather salvation-based works.

> This isn't works-based salvation,
> but rather salvation-based works.

The fruit of your life will reveal whether you are truly rooted in Christ or rooted in the world. Scripture says that "you will know them by their fruits" (Matthew 7:16, NKJV). By your actions and how you live, people will know what's in your heart. The Bible talks about the fruit of the Spirit and fruit of the flesh. So ask yourself right now: *How's my fruit? How's my joy? How's my peace? How's my patience? How's my kindness?*

If we are honest, a lot of us have more fruit of the flesh than we do of the Spirit. Our fruit looks more like control, selfishness, anxiety, impatience . . . and we look more like the world than we do Jesus.

Recently Grant and I had a work trip in California, which made for a long travel day. We had two connecting flights, and one had gotten delayed. By the time we arrived at our final airport, we were so hungry. And when I get hungry, I get hangry. When I am tired or haven't eaten, I have to pray extra hard for the Spirit to fill me and lead me. But we couldn't eat right away because we were on a tight timeline and needed to get our rental car. For some unknown reason, the rental car company kept sending people, including us, to the wrong place to pick up cars. So we dragged our bags all over the airport only to be sent to the wrong place. We were frustrated, but we held it together when we went back to the rental car desk.

Thankfully, the lady who served us was full of joy and tried to help us out. At the counter next to us, a woman was practically screaming at another worker, letting him have it for the long wait and miscommunication. Our sweet agent looked at us and smiled, saying, "The joy of the Lord is our strength." We smiled back and Grant said, "I had a feeling you were a Christian. You have so much joy and peace!" The woman next to us went from screaming at the worker to screaming at us, "I'M A CHRISTIAN TOO!"

We couldn't believe it. Her poor husband just stood beside her, looking down at the ground. Grant and I nodded, and he said, "That's awesome!"

When we got in the car, I looked at him with wide eyes and

said, "I think we have a different understanding of what it means to be a *Christian*."

I'm not here to judge her. I know I have had bad days and angry outbursts when tired and hungry, but her fruit was pretty obvious. Nothing about her choices in that moment and in her interactions lined up with what it looks like to be a true follower of Jesus.

Maybe you are wondering, is it even possible to fully commit to following Jesus? Is it possible to stay true in the world we live in today? To live the life God has called us to live? I will be honest with you—on your own, no. It is straight-up impossible. But with the help, guidance, and leadership of the Holy Spirit, nothing is impossible.

Like we read earlier in John 15, Jesus talks about how we can do nothing apart from Him. And, oh goodness, have I seen that to be true! In that passage, Jesus calls Himself the vine and says that we are the branches. When we're attached to Him, abiding in Him, relying on Him, we are fruitful and are connected to the source of life.

But have you ever passed by a branch disconnected from the tree? What do you notice? It's dead, not bearing fruit or life. The only way we experience and give the fruit of the Spirit—love, joy, peace, patience, kindness, goodness, faithfulness, gentleness, and self-control—is by staying attached to the vine.

We can't stay true without Him and His Spirit. Scripture repeatedly tells us that the Holy Spirit leads us in where to go, when to go, and how to go. In the Old Testament, God's Spirit was often manifested in fire or wind or some big revealing.

As awesome as that is, what's even greater is that because of Jesus's life, death, and resurrection, we don't have to rely on a cloud or fire or burning bush. We can have God's Spirit *inside* us, guiding us, leading us, and showing us the way.

It's time for us to step out of those toxic fumes, like Grant and I did with that gas leak, and step into life-giving fresh air. It's not enough for the truth to stay in our minds and hearts. Our feet must follow the truth so our lives reflect it.

In the next few chapters we will get more practical with how we can apply truth to our everyday lives, and together we will tackle how to overcome obstacles with a "dare to do" mindset, empowering us to live free and true.

DARE TO DO

If you answered the "one through ten" question in this chapter with anything below a ten, or if you felt convicted by the end of this chapter because you don't have a relationship with Jesus, are you ready to change that? If you are, then pray this prayer: Lord, I need You. I am a sinner and I need a Savior. I repent of my sins and surrender my life. I believe that Jesus died on the cross for my sins and then rose from the dead three days later. I believe in my heart and confess with my mouth that Jesus Christ is Lord, and today I make You the Lord of my life. I give You all of me. Body, soul, and spirit, I am Yours. In Jesus's name, amen.

9

DARE TO LIVE IN PRAYER

I prayed and my warts went away.

Let me start by saying, I grew up knowing all about Jesus. When I was young, around seven years old, I encountered the power of the Holy Spirit. Later, I got baptized. My relationship with Jesus from a young age was full of genuine passion and faith. I would share the good news of Jesus with random strangers. I was involved in Christian drama programs and sign language and choir at my church. I even witnessed miracles and healings. One time a lady I had never met asked me to pray over her body because she had some form of skin disease, and it caused her pain and shame. I prayed over her in great faith. The next week at church she came running up to me, exclaiming that she had been healed after our encounter. I was amazed at how great my God is.

I once prayed over my legs that had warts all over them. We had tried everything: Band-Aids, freezing them off, and even shaving them down. We tried the creams. Nothing seemed to work. So I decided it was time for God to intervene. I prayed over my knees and those stubborn warts in Jesus's name. The next morning, they were gone!

I grew up experiencing the power of prayer and how faith can quite literally move mountains—that there was nothing impossible for my God. I witnessed the miracles myself. My family would often joke with me about my love for prayer, saying that when they asked me to pray before a meal, all the food would get cold before I finished. Maybe they were right, but each vegetable, slice of meat, and roll was blessed before going into their bodies! I had an unashamed, persistent, and intimate prayer life. I never prayed hesitantly, in fear, or uncertain if my God could move—I knew He could.

But as I got older and started caring more about acceptance and the approval of people, my relationship with Jesus dwindled to surface-level religion. I stopped praying passionate and powerful prayers. I stopped expecting, in great faith, for God to move like He once did.

I started caring about the label on my clothes more than wearing my true God-given identity. I cared more about which boys were chasing me than I did about chasing Jesus with all my heart. I cared more about fitting in with the cool crowd than being set apart and on mission to reach the lost. In that late middle-school and high-school season of my life, my prayer life was nonexistent, other than the occasional bedtime prayers or family prayers before dinner.

Even heading into college, my faith life remained the same. College was the first time I had ever been fully on my own. I was getting to hang out late with boys and go out with friends without being asked by my mom, "Where are you going?" or by my dad, "What are you wearing?" This freedom led to tension in my heart about who I wanted to be and what kind of life I wanted to live. It led me to ask myself, "What do *I* believe? Who is Jesus to *me*?" I knew what my parents believed, but I needed to know what my own beliefs were. It was the first time in my life that I really had to choose.

One day when I was all alone in my dorm room, I began to cry out to God. I remembered what it was like when I was young: how close I felt to Him and the joy and peace I had. Now that I had all this "freedom" to do whatever I wanted, it didn't feel like what I thought it would. I felt holes in my heart that longed to be filled. I felt lonely and confused about who I was and what my purpose in life was. So I began to pray. I prayed with a genuine and broken heart, "God, I need You. I am lost. I don't want to play games with You anymore. I want to go all in and have a true relationship with You." It was at that moment I felt something shift. Not in my circumstances, at least not immediately, but something in my heart felt lighter and full of hope. I started to pray every day. Even though I didn't have real community at the time, God became my best friend.

In the second semester, I decided to join a college girls' small group. One night they issued a challenge—and I love a good challenge—to join our church in twenty-one days of prayer and fasting. Not one to back down, I committed. So, I set my alarm for five o'clock every morning and went to the church to pray for an hour straight. At first, I wondered, *How is this going to work? What am I going to say for an hour?*

And I'll be honest, at first I didn't have a whole lot to say to

God. An hour was a long time. I wondered, *Do I just ramble?* But I stayed in it. I kept showing up every morning. And something crazy happened. By the end of the twenty-one days, an hour wasn't enough time! My love and passion for connecting with God returned. I could've kept praying for hours. And I didn't want the twenty-one days to come to an end.

Maybe the way you feel about prayer is exactly like I did at the beginning of that challenge: intimidated, a little awkward, and unsure of exactly what to say or do. You're not alone in that. Most people know they should pray, but they don't. Remember how in the first half of this book we talked about lies that bind you and truth that frees you? Well, the enemy whispers lies that make you feel unworthy to pray, scared to pray, or too busy to pray. But the truth is that you were made to stay in constant communication with your creator.

A lot of people don't pray because they feel it's awkward or uncomfortable or intimidating. And it might be at first. When I was "rusty" in my prayer life, I felt the same way. But the more I did it, the more I realized I was made for this. And that I desperately needed it. To this day, prayer is my favorite way to connect with God. I learned that it wasn't just about talking, but also about listening. Prayer wasn't about what I could get from God; it was about being with God.

> Prayer wasn't about what I could get from God;
> it was about being with God.

I have seen prayer change things. I have seen prayer change people. I have seen prayer change me. Even when Grant and

I first got married, I would get on my knees and plead in prayer for the Lord to change some things about Grant to help him love me better and meet my expectations. But then something unexpected happened. It wasn't the circumstance or Grant that changed. It was *me*.

I have continued to learn more about prayer the longer I have been walking with Jesus. Prayer is not just something we do; it's something done to us. Prayer is powerful and effective. Prayer is intimate and connects us to God. Prayer is not an event, it's a lifestyle. It's not reserved for pastors and perfect Christians; it's for everyone. We are told all throughout Scripture to never stop praying.

> Prayer is not just something we do;
> it's something done to us.

So I ask you, how would you describe your prayer life? How often do you pray? What do you pray about? Do you have confidence that God will answer your prayers? What leads you to pray? What keeps you from praying?

Sometimes people say they don't have the time to pray. But the truth is, we don't have time *not* to pray. A lot of us do everything *but* pray. We talk about what's going on in the world, read about it, listen to podcasts about it, complain about it, or try to control it . . . when the best thing we could do is pray. Communion and connection with God fuels everything we do.

When I think back through my life over the last ten years, I have no idea who or where I would be without prayer. I can't confidently say I would be writing this book, or that I would have met and married my husband, or that I would be holding my newborn baby. I mean, even my time on *The Bachelor* would have been unbearable—impossible even—without prayer! The criticism and the pressure were so intense. I'd pray, "God, what do I say now? What do I do? What's my role here?" You might think reality TV and God don't mix. I understand that perspective. And personally, I wouldn't recommend going on a reality TV show or even watching one. But the truth is, God is everywhere and anywhere. Anyplace and anytime works for God. It doesn't matter who you are or where you are. In the book of James in chapter 5 it talks about when and how we should pray. *Are you in trouble?* Pray. *Are you happy?* Pray and praise. *Is anyone sick?* Gather people together and pray. It says, "The prayer of a righteous person is powerful and effective" (verse 16).

I have seen in my life that it is impossible to defeat the devil's schemes—daring to be true—without praying truth. So when should we pray? Always. In all circumstances—whether you're sick, healthy, happy, or suffering—all throughout your day.

PRAYER PROBLEMS

I believe one of the most powerful tools we've been given as Christians is prayer. It's how we stay connected to our Source. I'm talking about more than the before-meal prayers or night-night prayers, more than the vague, "Lord, be with me." (He is always with us.) I'm talking deep, intimate, powerful, passionate, Spirit-filled, Scripture-breathed prayers. Prayer is where your spiritual battery gets charged. Your heart and soul are fed by that interaction. Prayer is a lifestyle, a continual conversation, and a way to grow your relationship intimately.

If I asked you why you don't pray, what would you say? I think the three most common reasons people don't pray is because they think they don't know how, they're too busy, or they don't understand the privilege it is. Let's look at each of these in more detail.

"I don't know how to talk to God."

So often when people are asked to pray, they think or say, "Oh, I'm not very good at prayer." I can see the shame they carry as they say it. Prayer isn't meant to cause shame; it's meant to inspire faith. Prayer isn't about us or how we look or sound doing it; it's all about Jesus and thanking Him for what He's done and who He is. He wants an honest, genuine, and pure heart to sit with Him, seek Him, and praise Him.

A conversation with God doesn't need to be formal. He doesn't want an inauthentic performance from you. He just wants you—the real you. After all, you can't get deep with someone if you are pretending and performing. The good news is you don't need the perfect words, because prayer is not about the words you are saying; it's about your heart behind them.

Even if your prayer is only "Thank You, Jesus for saving me! Oh, how I need You, Lord. Show me how to love You today!" Even if it's a fraction of that, He just wants *you*.

In the same way that a first date can be awkward, your prayer life can make you feel uneasy. And if you start praying out loud, you might even feel crazy. But like in a relationship, after spending enough time together, things get much more comfortable. The more you grow in intimacy in your relationship, you will begin to realize the power and purpose of communication.

The same way you talk to a friend or someone you love, that's how you talk with God. And then you listen. It would be weird and wrong if, in my marriage, I only talked about myself. If I never asked my husband anything, never listened to him, or never sought to pursue him out of genuine love and affection, you would question the depth and intimacy of our relationship. In the same way, with God, it shouldn't just be you talking. And it shouldn't be centered only around you and your wants.

For some, prayer is intimidating and evokes a feeling of being ashamed. If you feel unworthy to go to God, remember: That is the enemy talking, and we rebuke him with the truth! The Bible says that as His children, we can "approach God's throne of grace with confidence" (Hebrews 4:16). That means we don't have to be afraid or ashamed. We can go to God ourselves. We don't need a priest or pastor to talk to God for us. Jesus and His finished work on the cross made it possible for us to come into God's presence with joy and confidence.

No matter your past, how you were raised, or what your experience with prayer has been, you can choose to approach God with confidence from this day forward. You don't have to work your way to Him, to earn favor by how good your prayers sound, or to strive for belonging. You are already accepted and loved.

When you take the focus off you, how you sound, and all your problems, and instead make your prayers all about God and who He is and what He has given you, it changes everything! Our prayers connect us to Him, remind us of how big He is and small we are, creating a need and dependence on Him.

"I'm too busy to pray."

Another reason people struggle in their prayer life is because they think they don't have time. The truth is that we will never naturally drift toward holiness and godliness; rather we will drift toward sin, worldliness, and selfishness. We can't just go into our day leaving it up to chance whether we "have time" for prayer. No, we must make it a priority, a nonnegotiable. Rather than letting your day decide what your time with Jesus looks like, *you* decide what your time with Jesus will look like. Life doesn't just happen to you. You aren't a victim to your schedule and busyness.

I remember one day when I was stressed, complaining about how I didn't have time to sit in quiet places with Jesus, my husband reminded me, "Madi, you do realize you have control over your choices and what your day looks like, right?" He was right. There may be a long, demanding list of to-dos. I realized it wasn't about seeing if God could fit in my to-do list, but rather realizing I can't do anything without Him. You choose what's important to you. You make time for what matters to you.

Busyness is just an excuse. We can all choose to make prayer a priority. That said, I recognize there are some seasons that our prayer time might look different. My prayer time as a single woman looked wildly different from my prayer time as a new mom. In singleness, I would sit on my bedroom floor alone for hours and cry out to God. Now I might be praying and praising God while breastfeeding. Another day might look like singing psalms over my little one. Other days, during nap time or when Grant is home, I might have longer time for prayer. Some days, I even have sporadic moments where I just cry out to God, "I need You, Lord!" Life might look different in certain seasons, but that isn't an excuse to not pray.

Scripture says to "pray continually," and that wasn't only addressed to singles and retired folk. Imagine if it said, "Pray continually, unless you are a new mom, or you're in your twenties and trying to earn a promotion, or unless you are a working father trying to provide for your family." Honestly, we probably need prayer in those seasons even more. Praying continually isn't based on circumstance; it's a choice, and we all have the choice.

Praying continually isn't based on circumstance;
it's a choice, and we all have the choice.

Think about what has gotten in the way of your prayer life. Is it busyness, apathy, feeling stressed? Busyness shouldn't be on the list—you can't afford *not* to pray. Sure, your time is limited, but finding time for prayer should be nonnegotiable. We make time for what's important.

"I had no idea how powerful prayer could be."

The other day I saw a video of an ex-satanist sharing her testimony of how Jesus had radically saved her and changed her life. She also explained that when she was a satanist and witch, day and night she would make it her goal to ruin Christians' lives. She was part of a satanic cult that would get together and pray to demons and call down curses on Christians and track them down. Just as I was starting to get terrified, wondering if some satanist might be hunting me down too, she said, "The crazy thing was that we couldn't hurt or get near Christians that were continuously praying. It would make the demons so mad!"

She said it looked like there was some type of force field around them. I imagine it like in the movie *The Incredibles*, where Violet's superpower was an invisible force field that protected whomever she was around. That is a picture of what our prayers do. They create a force field of power and protection around us and those for whom we intercede.

Grant has reminded me often that the enemy is after my prayer life. Satan hates when I pray. So he will use everything he can—busyness, distraction, temptation, or even the feeling of apathy—so that I don't pray. And he will do the same thing to you. Remember, he hates you. He wants you to stay bound. He may even be okay with you knowing the truth. But he really freaks out when you begin to follow and live out the truth. He doesn't want you free or on mission to free others.

Prayer is our first line of defense against any attack. It's something we do to align ourselves with the One who is so much greater than we are. We're trusting in God's providence and power. Talking with God happens here and now and always. There is always prayer going on. We're joining in a chorus.

Prayer does something in the supernatural realm we can't even see. It's earth meeting heaven. When we come into agreement with the Word of God and pray in the name of Jesus, it is powerful and effective. A great example of this happened in the Gospels when a young boy was possessed by a demon and the disciples tried to cast out the demon but couldn't get it out. Jesus cast out the demon and responded, "This kind can come out only by prayer" (Mark 9:29). Prayer isn't supposed to be pretty. Prayer is powerful. If you want to frolic in the fields with Jesus and pray, go for it. But also know that prayer is meant to be a battlefield, that it can push back darkness and bring us into agreement with the light and power of Jesus Christ.

One of my favorite pastors, Jentezen Franklin, calls this kind of consistent praying "prevailing" prayer. He says, "Prevailing prayer is not 'foxhole praying,' when you only pray when you get in trouble. Prevailing prayer is that consistent, insistent, continual life of communication with God. It's not something you *do;* it's a part of who you *are.* . . . With that kind of life of prayer you will know victory. Everything God wants to do is linked to prayer."*

Prayer builds an intimate relationship with God, strengthens us in times of temptation, and gives us courage and confidence when facing life's challenges. It is a source of healing, both emotional and physical. Prayer is how we connect the natural to the supernatural, and it's one of the greatest tools we have been given to fight off our enemy and push back darkness.

If you are feeling bound, weary, heavy, hurt, broken, lost, confused, burdened, or weighed down, prayer is your next step. All throughout Scripture, in both the Old Testament and New Testament, we are given examples of times a righteous person prayed in great faith and then miracles happened: Rain came in the midst of a drought, armies were thwarted and rerouted, nations were saved, people healed, chains broken, relationships restored, and so much more.

Maybe you are like, "Madi, I get it. The enemy doesn't want me to pray. And I need to pray. But *how* do I do it?"

A PRACTICAL PRAYER PLAN

Now that we are in our dare chapters, let's get practical and act on the things we know are true. We all know prayer is important and that we should pray more; however, many of us stop there. That changes today. Today, *we pray more*. Not tomorrow. Not someday. Today!

* Jentezen Franklin, *The Spirit of Python: Exposing Satan's Plan to Squeeze the Life Out of You* (Charisma House, 2013), 155.

As powerful and spiritual as prayer is, it's also practical. When we don't create a non-negotiable, disciplined schedule, we set ourselves up for failure. Most of the time the urgent things in our lives—rather than the important ones—take our time and energy. In order to be a person of prayer, you have to create a prayer plan. Without a plan, your prayer life will be left to chance, dependent on your emotions—which means it'll be inconsistent and maybe even nonexistent. The point of prayer is connection. But the key to maintaining that connection is consistency.

For me, what makes the most difference in my prayer life is starting my day with God. I have a prayer closet. It's a tiny space—literally a *closet*. I leave my phone outside the room, and I remove distractions and get still before God. Handwritten prayers fill the walls. I keep my Bible open, and I light a candle. I kneel or sit or lie; I pace around or yell or cry—it doesn't matter what I do because nobody but God is watching. Prayer isn't for an audience—it's an intimate thing. Before I had a closet, I prayed in the car. I'd just drive and talk with God. I'd sing and sob and talk to God to my heart's content. The more I seek Him and make the space for Him, the closer we get. But my prayers to God and with God aren't just limited to my mornings. All day long, I am talking to God, talking about God, or thinking about Him. We stay in constant communication.

Here's the thing, my prayer life didn't start that way. I developed a practical prayer plan and I stuck to it.

How can you have a consistent prayer life? Consider these three P's:

1. **Place.** I have my prayer closet. If I'm traveling, I create a space wherever I am. I bring my routine with me. You can pray in your room, your closet, on a walk, in your car, the shower, your couch, wherever. Find a place where you can be uninterrupted and not self-conscious.

2. **Posture.** Intentional conversations don't happen randomly. They take focus. So find a posture. Sit cross-legged on the floor or kneel. Or stand with your hands uplifted or sit with them quietly in your lap. You might even sit at a table and write in a journal. I start on my knees. I tend to be animated when I talk, so I might hop up and pace. I encourage you to pray out loud. It may seem a little weird at first, but it has been a game changer for me. It creates an awareness in your heart and body, and usually when I keep my prayers in my head, I get distracted or fall asleep.

3. **Plan.** Not just *when* you'll pray, but *how* you'll pray. Like anything else, if you go into it without a plan, it might not be effective or may even fail. My plan is to always begin with gratitude and thanksgiving, thanking God for who He is and all He has done and is doing. I call this "looking up." Next, I like to move into a time of confession and repentance, confessing any sin I know of in my life and asking God to purify my heart. I then pray Psalm 139:23–24, "Search me, God, and know my heart; test me and know my anxious thoughts. See if there is any offensive way in me, and lead me in the way everlasting." I call this "looking in." Then I will pray my own personal and relational prayers, asking God for intercession in the matters closest to my heart. I write down names or dreams on a prayer

card and tape it to my wall. And to end my prayer time, I like to pray in alignment with God's heart as revealed in Scripture: praying for those who don't know Jesus, the abused, neglected, marginalized, abandoned, and for those in leadership and authority in our nation and world (our government, teachers, pastors, and parents). I call this "looking out."

That is my typical prayer plan. But sometimes I pray Scripture and just praise God. Sometimes I pray the Lord's Prayer. Sometimes I just cry out to God in repentance and sit in His presence. Although the plan could change, it's good to at least *have* a plan. My dad always used to say, "If you fail to plan, then you plan to fail." Without a plan, I have found myself just rambling to God or getting distracted or even falling asleep. Plans are good!

There are some things I have been praying and believing for years. I just keep praying in faith. Some prayers are answered quickly, and I rejoice greatly! God wants to hear what is on our hearts, and He desires to answer our prayers if they align with His will.

But prayer isn't just *about* us, and it isn't just *for* us. It's not a therapy session where we leave after we've said everything necessary to feel better. That's not true prayer. Prayer is connection. It's relational. It's talking and listening. The best example of how prayer holds benefits outside ourselves is found in Jesus.

Jesus fortified Himself with prayer often so that He could heal, teach, and love well. Spending time alone with God fueled Him. When His disciples noticed how prayer shaped Him, they asked Him to teach them to pray. That's how we got what we call the Lord's Prayer. It's in Matthew 6:9–13, and it's also a great framework to use in your own prayers.

Just like I prayed and my warts went away, what do you wish would go away in your life? Worry, anxiety, shame, relational tension, offense, sin addictions? Pray. Jesus showed us that even when we feel bound and overwhelmed, we should pray. Right before being crucified, Jesus prayed to God, overwhelmed with sorrow to the point of sweating drops of blood! No matter your circumstances or what you are believing God for in your life, this is your challenge: Take it to God. Not tomorrow or in the future. Now is the time to pray. I dare you!

DARE TO DO

Write out your own prayer plan and then commit
to twenty-one days of praying through it.

10

DARE TO LIVE PURE

My mom had the sex talk with me when I was nine years old.

We read through a Christian girls' book that talked about all the parts of a girl's body and what they were made for. It emphasized that God made all the parts for a purpose, and that our body was not to be freely shared with just anyone who wanted it. I'm pretty sure my face was red from the beginning of the book until my mom closed it. Talking about sex and body parts was weird and awkward.

Growing up in a small, Bible-Belt town and in an Assemblies of God church, I knew sex before marriage was a big no-no. It was almost taught like this was one of the worst sins, even though I didn't know why. I knew sex outside of marriage wasn't the "right thing to do," but there were moments where I resented that, questioned it, and tried to dance around purity as much as I could.

I realize saying the words "purity" or "purity culture" can elicit quite a reaction. Many have been hurt by purity culture because of an upbringing or institution that focused solely on rules and duties without communicating the true heart and purpose of purity. Others have been hurt by purity culture because they fell into sexual sin and then were judged or turned away from the church. Some feel hurt because they experienced things sexually against their will, and they wondered if that meant they were impure. Others partially pursued purity, thinking it was only about "not having sex," but thought everything else sexual was fair game. Others have pursued purity out of fear or obligation And some wanted to honor God because they understood the *why* behind purity.

Wherever you stand on this topic and whatever has happened until this point in your life, I want you to know you are welcome and wanted here. This is a safe space for you. Just know that we have all made mistakes in our lives and have lived impurely, whether in body, mind, or heart.

As for me, I made the decision to wait to have sex until I was married. But to be honest with you, I chose purity because I felt like I had to. Part of me didn't want God to be mad at me, and the other part of me pridefully wanted to be able to say I had my virgin card. And then later I became the person who partially pursued purity, who abstained from sex yet lived impurely in other ways. I pushed boundaries physically with my boyfriends and I watched pornography, which led to masturbation, in secret. Sure, I could "hang my hat" on not having sex, but I was still living in sexual sin, had an impure heart, and was being ruled by a spirit of lust.

So many of us have a completely wrong or unclear view or understanding of what purity really is. Maybe it's a result of our church, our parents' sex talks, an exposure to porn early on, judgment we received from another Christian or church, or because no one ever really explained to us what true purity is.

Until my college years, I had a fear-based and reputation-based understanding of purity. I wanted to make my parents proud and set a good example for my sisters. I wanted to be the "good Christian girl." And I thought God would bless me more if I saved myself for marriage and followed all His "rules." Pursuing purity in my mind was looking clean and put together on the outside—being able to say, "I'm still a virgin." Yet all the while I was struggling with secret sin and living an impure life.

But something changed during my freshman year of college. I fell in love with a good God who was pure and holy. And because I loved Him, wanted to be like Him, and wanted to follow Him, I wanted to be pure and holy too. I also noticed that when I pursued purity, it led to greater intimacy with God and the blessing of peace, confidence, security, and purpose. Yet the moments I fell back into sexual sin or followed sinful thoughts and cravings, it led to anxiety, shame, insecurity, and hopelessness. That was when I realized God calls us to be pure because it's for our best interest. Living in purity leads to living in freedom. And although that's not what the world and culture preach—because sexual sin has become so normalized—it's true that purity leads to freedom while impurity leads to bondage.

Living in purity leads to living in freedom.

So my prayer for you is that as you read this chapter, you feel no shame or judgment. Instead, I hope you feel a sense of conviction and calling to pursue purity because it leads to more of Him. If you haven't lived in purity up until this point in your life, you can choose today to pursue purity. Your past is your past for a reason. You can't change it. But you can change the decisions you make right now—and that could lead to a future in God's will and presence.

My hope is that you see that purity is more about the posture of our hearts than bodily action or inaction. And that is a gift, not a curse. Purity is a blessing God wants to give you, not something He wants to withhold from you.

IT'S A HEART THING

Have you ever shoved all your dirty clothes under the bed to make it seem like your room was clean? Well, I did that a lot growing up. My mom would ask me to clean my room and she would tell me that my dad was going to come up and check to make sure it was clean. So what would I do? I would quickly shove all my dirty clothes under the bed and into drawers. When my dad would look in my room and see clean floors and a made bed, he would give me the thumbs-up and walk away. Because at quick glance, it looked really clean. But the reality was that all the clutter and mess was just moved to a different place, a hidden place.

This is a good representation of the difference between

purity and cleanliness. Purity is what lies hidden beneath the bed, and cleanliness is simply what people see. As believers, many of us have been taught to wrongly place an emphasis on outward cleanliness (which is still important!) rather than a heart that is spotless and pure.

In Matthew 5:8, it says "Blessed are the pure in heart, for they will see God." Notice it doesn't say pure in body. No, Jesus expands the expectation of purity. Purity is not just a measure of abstinence and having your "virgin card." It is rather a descriptor of the very core of a person—the heart.

Rarely does anyone talk about the heart, the why and purpose of purity, and the gift of it. We think if we look like we have it together on the outside, that's what God really cares about. Let's admit that can be what the church often focuses on—having a good and clean reputation. Yet, all the while there is hidden and secret sin. And Jesus speaks to this issue in Matthew 23:25–28:

> Woe to you, teachers of the law and Pharisees, you hypocrites! You clean the outside of the cup and dish, but inside they are full of greed and self-indulgence. . . . First clean the inside of the cup and dish, and then the outside also will be clean. . . . You are like whitewashed tombs, which look beautiful on the outside but on the inside are full of the bones of the dead and everything unclean. In the same way, on the outside you appear to people as righteous but on the inside you are full of hypocrisy and wickedness.

If we are all honest, there are some of us that look cleaned up on the outside, but on the inside our hearts are full of sin and secrets. Jesus understood something we often miss. Everything—the decisions we make, the thoughts we think, and the words we say—flows from what lies within our hearts. That's why the Bible says in Proverbs 4:23, "Above all else, guard your heart, for everything you do flows from it." It's like Jesus wanted us all to understand a very important principle: The heart is everything. What's in your heart will direct your life.

If we focus only on the hands, the eyes, the feet, and the things that are seen, but never get to the heart, it's all for nothing. Purity is a posture of the heart, not just a set of rules to follow.

PURITY BLOCKERS

Have you ever heard of beta blockers? Although I have never found a need for them myself, I find them to be interesting and relatable to what we are talking about. Beta blockers are used to lower blood pressure and protect someone against a heart attack. They work by slowing down the heart by blocking the release of stress hormones like adrenaline. The purpose of beta blockers is to keep something bad from happening.

Although you may not need beta blockers, many of us experience what I like to call "purity blockers." Purity blockers prevent us from walking in God's will and experiencing His best for our lives. In other words, unlike beta blockers, they're keeping *good* things from happening. The enemy often uses these purity blockers as obstacles to keep us from walking in purity and living the lives of *more* that God created us for.

We have talked a lot throughout this book about the enemy's lies—that his goal is to keep us tangled up and trapped in our sin and shame. One of the greatest ways he does this is by attacking our purity. Looking at our world today, many of us have fallen for Satan's lies when it comes to our bodies, sexuality, and relationships. We believe lies about our bodies—that we have to look a certain way—or lies about our relationships— that we have to do certain things to be loved or accepted. Satan disguises himself as a messenger of light and love. Even when it comes to our sexuality, think about the mantra of today: "Love is love." That idea feels inclusive, accepting, and even loving, but it doesn't lead to a life that offers freedom—it leads to bondage. These lies block us from true freedom and the real love we were made for.

For Scripture says in 1 John 4:8, "God is love." The enemy knows this and that is why he tries to twist and pervert the truth to confuse us into believing that we can find love outside of God and outside of God's design.

Back when I was enslaved to pornography, I was confused on what love was, who I was attracted to, what sex was, and what orgasms should be. I am not here to shame you or make you feel bad about decisions you have made up until this point. I too have believed the enemy's lies about sexuality and purity. I too have battled shame and falling into the same temptation again and again, wondering if I would ever be able to break free and if there was any hope for me.

And if that's you, I want to say there is hope. Just like beta blockers, purity blockers only work if you take them. Satan wants you to believe the lie that "If you feel it you have to follow it." He says to just follow your feelings because those feelings are normal, can be trusted, and should be followed. He makes us believe that when temptation comes, we have to give in. But that is not what the Bible says in 1 Corinthians 10:13. "No temptation has overtaken you except what is common to mankind. And God is faithful; he will not let you be tempted beyond what you can bear. But when you are tempted, he will also provide a way out so that you can endure it."

For the longest time, I felt like I had to give in to sin. And whenever temptation came, I thought I was a slave to my cravings and desires. But this verse tells me that falling for temptation is a choice. And that there will always be a way out. There will always be an option to choose purity.

But that doesn't mean it will be easy. The enemy says, "If it makes you feel good, do it"—as if you're meant to follow everything that feels pleasurable, normal, and natural to your body. But Truth says those of us who are in Christ are to continually die to the self and crucify our flesh. Following our flesh leads to death, but living by the Spirit leads to life and peace. We have to intentionally die to our lustful desires.

The truth is, having sexual feelings and longings is not wrong. God created our bodies. Sex was God's idea, and He is the inventor of pleasure. He created orgasms. He put the nerve endings where they are. He created sex and sexual acts within the context of marriage to lead to a bonding union, pleasurable sensation, and worshipful experience. God's design is not flawed. And when it is experienced the right way, it is beautiful.

When we climax, our brain creates a bond to our surroundings—which is meant to unify and inspire worship when pursued in marriage. But when we fall for the enemy's deception and we masturbate to porn, fantasies, or steamy romance novels, we are bonding with whatever is around us and in front of us. When we have sexual experiences with another person who is not our spouse, we are creating soul ties with that person. And it isn't the right kind of tie that leads to unity and freedom. It is the kind of tie that leads to bondage.

For me, when I learned that purity was possible, it changed everything. As I began in my own life to believe the truth of God's Word about my sexuality, and I confessed to other believers and had them hold me accountable, I learned that purity is possible. And it is for you too.

DARE TO LIVE PURE

If you watch sports, you will notice that there is always a defense and an offense. There is always a goal to score and a time to defend to keep the other team from scoring. When I played basketball, defense was always my favorite. I loved trying with all I had to keep the other team from scoring. But the game would be pointless if my team only played defense, if we never tried to actually score. In sports you need *both* a good defense and offense to win the game. Well, just like in sports, when it comes to living pure and living free, you need a good defense and offense. Let me unpack what I mean.

For a lot of us, when we think about purity we only think about defense: "Don't have sex!" or "Stay away from the couch!" We have only focused on fleeing temptation. But to live in purity, there is also an offense: pursuing holiness.

When I have focused only on fleeing, what followed was either religion or rebellion. I either walked in self-righteousness— making everything all about me, my reputation, and what I could do. Or I fell back into sin and rebelled against God and His calling on my life. But once I realized the importance of pursuing, I was able to pursue purity to grow my relationship with Jesus, not my reputation. After I confessed to other believers and began to pursue God with all my heart, I realized it became even easier to flee from things that used to enslave and bind me.

Second Timothy 2:22 says, "Flee also youthful lusts; but pursue righteousness, faith, love, peace with those who call on the Lord out of a pure heart" (NKJV). I think the reason so many of us fail at living in purity is because we don't abide by both halves of this verse. It doesn't just stop at *flee*. It goes on to say *but pursue*. Yes, flee from sin and lust, but also pursue righteousness, faith, love, and peace with those who call upon the Lord out of a pure heart. The true root of our purity stems from our pursuit of God.

Let's explore four practical ways we can pursue a life of purity.

1. Confess for healing.

I have talked multiple times throughout this book about the importance of confession. For me, that was my first step to finally breaking free from sexual sin. We do that by first confessing to God in repentance, asking Him to forgive us of our sins, and committing to a life of honor and holiness. Then we confess to a godly friend or mentor and have them pray over us so that we may be healed. Many of us pray and ask God for forgiveness without confessing to others. We then go on living without anyone holding us accountable, which can lead to more shame or more sin. But we are told in the Bible that confession to other believers is how healing is found. James 5:16 says, "Therefore confess your sins to each other and pray for each other so that you may be healed. The prayer of a righteous person is powerful and effective." In other words, healing requires revealing. When I finally brought my sin and secrets into the light and told a friend, that was when I began to truly experience the power of the gospel: God's forgiveness, love, mercy, and freedom.

You may still have a lot of questions around confession. I know I did. *Who do I confess to?* Someone who loves both God and you—a friend, a parent, or a church leader of the same gender. *What should I confess?* Well, any and every sin. But since we are focusing on purity and sexual sin, here are a few: porn, masturbation, idolizing your body, sexual sin, sending out a naked picture, sexting, and anything else you can think of. *When should I confess?* Immediately, or as quickly as possible. Big sins don't start big; they start as small, unconfessed sins. *How should I confess?* Fast and fully. Tell everything, and don't hold anything back.

2. Cut off temptation triggers.

The root issue with most people battling lust and sexual sin addiction is that they choose to not flee from the very situations that cause them to fall into sin. This is the defensive side of things we were talking about earlier. In order to win the battle against lust and impurity, you have to have a good defense strategy, and the Bible is clear about what that strategy should look like. Matthew 5:30 says, "If your right hand causes you to stumble, cut it off and throw it away. It is better for you to lose one part of your body than for your whole body to go into hell." The first step to being victorious in this area is to *identify the "hand" in your life.* It may be your Xbox, YouTube, steamy romance novels, racy shows or movies, Instagram, Snapchat, or other social media or online sites that are feeding those cravings. Once you identify it, *cut it off.*

We can't flirt with sin or simply tolerate it. We have to cut it off, and that means being intentional and intense with it. If necessary, delete Instagram, cancel your Netflix subscription, get a flip phone, have a friend who has access to all your social media accounts and search history—whatever it takes. Identify the trigger to your sin and cut it off. Kill sin, or sin will kill you.

3. Find accountability and godly community.

We can't pursue purity alone. And we definitely can't pursue purity when we're doing life with impure people. Real friends don't push you to sin; real friends push you to God. The right friends don't corrupt your character; the right friends make your character look more like Jesus. Proverbs 13:20 says, "Whoever walks with the wise becomes wise, but the companion of fools will suffer harm" (ESV).

Friends are like the flu; they are contagious. And you will catch what they have. If they're chasing after righteousness, you're going to catch that. If they're pursuing purity, you're going to catch that. If they are living a life of sin and compromise, you are going to catch that. Put yourself in a group of people who are pursuing Jesus and living in purity.

Then decide on sexual boundaries for your life ahead of time, with accountability. Don't wait until you get in the heat of the moment to make decisions, because your feelings and body will lie to you. Once you have decided your boundaries, bring accountability and mentorship into it.

Not only should godly friends be a safe place to confess to when you fall into sin, they should also be the ones holding you accountable to keep you from falling into sin in the first place. When Grant and I were dating, we learned really fast that the couch was not a good place for us—too tempting. So we created a contract that listed our boundaries and nonnegotiables when it came to pursuing purity in our relationship, and we signed it and then sent it to our accountability partners to hold us to it.

We were never meant to do this Christian life alone, and in the next chapter we are going to talk about community and how we can find godly friends. But it is important for you to know that your pursuit of purity is deeply impacted by your community. Living in isolation and secrecy is just as dangerous as doing life with people who are living impure and ungodly lives. We need godly people around us in our pursuit of purity. Paul told Timothy to pursue purity with the right people, in 2 Timothy 2:22, "Flee the evil desires of youth and pursue righteousness, faith, love and peace, *along with those who call on the Lord out of a pure heart.*" Friends can influence your life toward purity or lust.

4. Pursue a relationship with God.

These first three things are all great, but if this fourth element is missing—if we aren't abiding in the presence of the Lord and growing our relationship with Him—then at some point we will burn out. If all we do is flee and focus on playing defense, we will fail. This is now our offense time. We have to score to win the game. And we do that by consistently abiding in the Word, in God's presence, in prayer, and in worship. Psalm 119:9–11 says, "How can a young person stay on the path of purity? By living according to your word. I seek you with all my heart; do not let me stray from your commands. I have hidden your word in my heart that I might not sin against you." We can't just focus on resisting the bad; we must also pursue the good. *Purity is not just fleeing from something, but also a pursuit of something.*

And as we pursue purity and truth more and more, our

discipline will develop into delight. It may not start out with delight right away. For most of us, discipline does not come naturally or easily. But when we discipline our minds and bodies, there is great satisfaction and fruit—holiness, intimacy with Jesus, and experiencing His purpose for our life.

THE PURPOSE OF PURITY

The point of purity is more than just refraining from sinful sexual pleasure. It's *much* more. *Purity is the path to God's presence.* The end goal of purity is not just about getting something; it's about being with Someone. As we talked about in the eternity chapter, Psalm 16:11 says, "You make known to me the path of life; you will fill me with joy in your presence, with eternal pleasures at your right hand."

Being in His presence is where fullness of joy is found. Pursuing purity leads us to see God, to encounter His presence. In His presence there is *fullness of joy,* in His presence there is *freedom,* in His presence there is *peace.* Everything we were hardwired for and what we deeply desire can only be found when we pursue purity.

For me, waiting until marriage was so worth it. That day I said "I do" to Grant was the day he got all of me: body, soul, and spirit. I was his completely. And I had saved it for him. And I commit to keep it his. But that wasn't even the best part. Making the commitment to save myself for marriage was more than just being able to give my body to my husband for my first time. Every day leading up to my wedding day, I got to be fully God's: body, soul, and spirit. I was His. No one else had me. He had all of me. And in being married, purity doesn't stop. I still have to pursue it. God still has all of me. And now Grant has all of me. But I have to continue to resist temptation, die to my sinful cravings, and pursue purity with all of my being.

And even if that hasn't been or currently isn't your story, it can be. Remember that the blood of Jesus washes us clean! He makes us brand new. We can all choose to commit to purity and give God our bodies fully, no matter the past. As you know because of all I have shared, my past was not perfectly pure, and Grant's wasn't either. We both had a past with sexual sin. And even if that hasn't been a struggle for you, we all have a past of impurity, even if just in our minds and hearts.

When we follow God's will for purity, we not only avoid the pain and shame that comes with extramarital sex and sexual acts, but we also experience greater depths of joy, peace, faith, love, and purpose. As you walk in God's will and in obedience, you will have freedom to experience the fullness of life. As I've said, I didn't always see purity as a gift or as the pathway to God's presence. But when my perception changed, everything changed. I was no longer pursuing purity because I wanted something *from* God but rather to be closer *to* God.

Purity is more than the physical. It's spiritual. Purity isn't just about the body. It's a heart posture. Purity is a lifestyle. It is a gift, not a curse. Purity is a calling, not just a command. Purity is not just something you "do." It's who you are . . . and *Whose* you are. You are a pure and holy believer. Because it's who He is.

DARE TO DO

From this day forward, I pledge to pursue purity and honor God's plan for my life, individually and in relationships. I promise to keep my mind and my body holy so that when I one day enter the covenant of marriage, I will be able to give my body, soul, and spirit completely to my spouse. I believe sexual intimacy is a gift from God that was designed within the context of marriage only. I pledge to not put myself in situations where I will be tempted, but to live above reproach. I will use the Bible as my standard to pursue purity and set boundaries, physically and spiritually, emotionally and relationally.

Signed,

Name: _____ Date: _____

11

DARE TO LIVE IN COMMUNITY

I got drunk and started counseling my lost friends.

Yeah, not my proudest moment. It was my first time ever drinking alcohol.

My young heart was hurting after I had found out I had gotten cheated on. I was so upset that I decided to get back at my boyfriend by getting drunk. Makes sense, right? Well, it did in my sixteen-year-old brain. The only reason I had access to any alcohol was because of the friends I was with. We were staying at the house of one of my friends, whose mom happened to be out of town. Her cabinet was full of all her favorite beverages. When my friends pulled out a bottle of vodka, I gave it a whiff and thought, *Why would anyone want to drink this? It smells like the rubbing alcohol the doctor uses to wipe down my skin before giving me a shot.*

But as all my friends started mixing drinks, and as my heart was aching and longing for some kind of pick-me-up, I decided to join them. We turned up loud music and started taking shots. I didn't quite know how shots worked. So, after the fifth one, I bragged to my friends that "I didn't feel a thing!" Little did I know, just thirty minutes later I would be slurring my words and walking funny.

The thing is, these friends didn't really know Jesus. They didn't grow up in a family that raised them to love and know Jesus like mine had. For years I had been trying to encourage my friends in their faith and had invited them to church, but they always blew me off. My mom told me to be careful spending time with them or they might rub off on me instead of my rubbing off on them. I rolled my eyes at the constant reminder: *Bad company will corrupt good character.*

Until this point, I had always turned down the drinks I was offered. I had tried my best to be the "good girl." But this night I was vulnerable and sad. This night I let the company around me impact my decisions and compromise my convictions. After realizing that the alcohol was making me feel different, I tried to override the guilt I was feeling and the sin I was committing by sharing the gospel with these girls—slurred words and all. I tried to encourage them that following Jesus was where true life and fun was found. And they listened but then responded, "But, Madi, we're all having so much fun right now!" When I heard the word "we," my heart sank. Instead of influencing them to Jesus, they were influencing me to sin.

I had compromised my character and hurt my witness. Not only was I making decisions I would go on to regret, but I also was confusing their understanding of what following Jesus looked like. That's when I realized my mom had been right all those times: *The company I keep will help me hold true to my convictions or push me to compromise them.* My friends will corrupt my character or challenge it to be even greater. My friends will push me to Jesus or to sin. There is no neutral ground.

We were made for community. The right kind of community. Godly community. Life will move in the direction of our relationships, forward or backward. And we will become like those we choose to surround ourselves with.

Remember what we talked about in the last chapter? Friends are like the flu. We will catch what they have. So, when we spend a lot of time around people who are constantly compromising and choosing to live in sin, we will catch that. Their symptoms will become our symptoms. And the opposite is true. If we spend a lot of time around people who are constantly pursuing Jesus and purity and godliness, we will catch that too!

It's also worth noting, isolation is just as dangerous. We weren't made to go through life alone. Going through life alone and isolated can be just as destructive as doing life with people who promote sin in our lives.

I have shared throughout this book how my life literally changed when I found godly friends. I wouldn't be where I am today and I wouldn't be doing what I am doing today—walking in my purpose and living deeply in my faith—if it weren't for my Jesus-loving friends. Not only have my friends carried me through some of the hardest times of my life, but they have also called me out of sin, pushed me to holiness, and helped me love Jesus more.

I'll never forget a moment when I was at dinner with three

of my closest friends when I was twenty-five and single (and quite tired of being single). I was ready to find a husband and get married. I had been dating one guy on and off, and I knew deep down he was not God's best for me. But I would try to justify the relationship every time, "Oh, there are way worse guys! He does at least love God . . ."

But after this dinner with my friends where we laughed until we cried, dreamed together, talked about what Jesus was teaching us, asked intentional and challenging questions, and encouraged each other and prayed for each other, I knew I needed to break up with him. I looked at them and said, "I want to marry someone who makes me love Jesus like you guys do." It was the truth. Every time after spending time with these friends, I left better than how I had shown up. I left feeling encouraged and closer to Jesus. I left feeling challenged and convicted. I left feeling seen and known. And I knew the man God had for me would be a man that would do the same.

And even today, I am so grateful for friends who don't let me settle when it comes to who God has called and created me to be. I am grateful for friends who celebrate me in my highs, carry me through my lows, and bring joy to my life in the everyday moments. I am thankful for friends who push me closer to Jesus.

And I want that for you too.

Why is community so important? It aligns with the very nature of God. God is communal: The Trinity—God the Father, Jesus the Son, and the Holy Spirit—is three in one. We were made *from* relationship, *for* relationship. Since we serve a communal God, we were made for community. The *right* community. Looking at the life of Jesus, we see He could have done His saving work and ministry all by Himself, but He chose to have a circle of friends. Living in community with other believers is how we participate in God's kingdom.

My dad always used to say, "Teamwork makes the dream work." And it's true. We can accomplish more when we do it together. I also love the saying, "If you want to go fast, go alone. If you want to go far, go with others." We want to go far. But for a lot of us, we never become all we could be, because we settle for isolation or ungodly friendships. Let's talk first about what often keeps us from godly and healthy friendships.

S.O.S: NO CONNECTION

Have you ever been in a situation where you have no cell service and your phone alerts you that you have "no connection"? This can get scary when we are alone at night or needing to get somewhere and don't have service. Our phone even tells us *how* scary by putting up the acronym "SOS" in the top right corner of our iPhone. SOS is an alert or signal for extreme danger or distress—usually we say it as a plea for help. Well, in the same way when it comes to our life and our relationships, we are in danger and distress when we lose connection.

Do you know what the most severe punishment is in prison, other than death itself? Solitary confinement. Shut off from all human connection, locked up in isolation. You will begin to lose your sanity and humanity.

Community can be something desired deep down, yet something not pursued because of our self-focused and social-media-obsessed culture. We have become individualized. Many of us have social media followers but not true friends. In our world, we have never had more access to connection with people, yet we feel so disconnected in our real-life relationships. This is particularly true in our country. The United States ranks number one as the world's most individualistic nation, so no wonder we feel so lonely.*

If we are honest with ourselves, most of us do not feel fully known, seen, or connected—or like we belong. Yet we long for connection because we were made for it. I'm not talking about social media connection that just requires a quick click to like or comment. I mean *real* connection. Connection that requires deeply intentional conversation, regular confession, and consistent quality time together.

The problem exists even in church. Nowadays we use social media, online sermons, and podcasts as our substitute for church and real community. This doesn't mean those things are sinful. I also have social media, listen to sermons, and watch podcasts. I even have my own podcast! However, these things are meant to be supplements, not substitutes. For me, listening to a sermon online is an addition to my time with God. Listening to a sermon does not replace going to church,

* "Individualistic Countries 2024," World Population Review, worldpopulationreview.com/country-rankings/individualistic-countries.

being involved in a small group and godly community, or finding a mentor or leader in my life that I can learn from and ask questions and have conversations with.

It's similar with this book. Though I am so glad you are reading, my hope is that you are encouraged to then dive deeper into *the* Book, the Word of God, on your own. I hope this book encourages you in your faith and challenges you to be all God has called you to be. But I pray it doesn't stop there, and instead it leads you to get plugged into a local church, to find friends who will continue to push you and encourage you in your faith hereafter.

As you know, the 2020 pandemic ushered in a whole new level of loneliness, isolation, and individualism. We were on lockdown. Churches shut down. Schools shut down. Workspaces shut down. People lost their sense of being around others in a life-giving, free, and normal way. For a time, being around people created fear and uncertainty, and it could even get you sick. Then after the pandemic passed, it was as if we forgot how to do life with people. We were so used to social distancing, which heightened our social anxiety and created an epidemic of real loneliness. Since then, connecting with people seems to take more effort and feel more awkward.

Not only have these factors had a negative effect on our ability to connect relationally with others, but our past wounds of relational hurt and rejection also complicate connection. I can speak from experience on this one.

In 2019, when I followed what I felt was a call by God to go on reality TV—*The Bachelor*—many didn't understand or agree with my decision. I honestly didn't either. But through a lot of prayer and talking with community, I made the decision to say yes with full peace and clarity. But there still came a lot of judgment and rejection. My then-church made it clear that their staff did not support my decision. I felt misunderstood, even by church friends I had done life with for years. What followed was gossip, harsh and hurtful comments, and the end of friendships. My reaction was bitterness toward the church. I was afraid to step into any church after that out of fear of getting rejected or judged again.

This led to years of not being plugged into a local church and having a lot of anger in my heart toward it. I'm not alone in this. A lot of people—maybe even you—have felt judged or hurt by the church. Whether it was from church members or pastors or just Christians in general, I am sorry. I know that church hurt and being deeply hurt by another believer are hard things to resolve in your heart.

This is still an insecurity and struggle for me today. The number of times I hear from other believers I meet who say to me, "Oh, you actually love God and know the Bible—that's so cool to see!" is just crazy. I will even have people confess to me that they judged me as a phony Christian for going on reality TV before getting to know me and seeing my heart up close.

What I realized was that after years of distancing myself and walking in bitterness toward the church, I was only hurting myself. I was only keeping myself from experiencing the full life Jesus wanted to give me. I finally experienced freedom after I got on FaceTime with one of the girls who I had really been hurt by, and I forgave her. I realized that Satan wants me bound by bitterness and shut off from the church. The enemy wants us fighting other believers instead of him, and many of us waste our time and energy fighting the wrong battles. We spend our time fighting people who hurt us, instead of the enemy who is behind it all. As Ephesians 6 tells us, "Our struggle is not against flesh and blood" (verse 12).

Unfortunately, because we are all human and sinful, we will fail and hurt one another. Just as I have been deeply hurt by people, I have deeply hurt others. People are going to disappoint us, and we will disappoint them. That is a part of life. *If we want to walk in true freedom, we can't let the pains of our past keep us from a free future.* And that is exactly what the enemy wants because he knows life change and freedom happen in relationships. Harboring bitterness, unforgiveness, and anger toward someone, no matter what they did to you, will only hurt you and keep you from what God has for you.

After I forgave my friend, I was able to get plugged back into a church, and I started to trust people again. That friend and I didn't go back to the relationship we once had—there were still some boundaries—but now there was nothing in either of us but love and forgiveness.

Church rejection is different from church accountability. Some people walk away from churches because the preacher calls out their sin and they don't like it, or because someone in their small group tells them what they don't want to hear. It's so easy to be offended by truth. But as we have learned, only the truth will set us free. We need truth spoken to us by friends, mentors, and pastors in order for us to be who God has called us to be. We need godly friends who care more about our souls than our feelings.

*We need godly friends who care more
about our souls than our feelings.*

There have been many situations I have seen within the church and within godly community when someone gets called out on their sin, and the person or couple ends up getting defensive and angry, and leaving the church or friend group completely. It shows what happens when all we want is for people to pity our sin, tell us what we want to hear, and just let us be.

I remember when I had a friend once tell me that I was selfish. Ouch! That wasn't fun to hear. I had a friend who told me I needed to forgive someone who had hurt me because it was ungodly for me to carry bitterness in my heart. I had another friend tell me that the way that I dressed wasn't godly and was confusing to those I witnessed to. I wanted to get defensive: "Well, you don't know! That's just your opinion." I'm sure the list of times that friends have confronted me on my sin and shortcomings could go on and on. But I'm now glad they did, because it made me a better follower of Jesus.

So, now we have addressed the fact that many of us have lost connection because of the enemy's lies or society's pull to individualism. But just like it's dangerous to lose connection driving on a dark road alone, it is dangerous to lose connection in a dark world alone.

FAITH-FILLED FRIENDSHIPS

One of my favorite stories in the Bible about faith-filled friendships might be the one in Luke 5:18–25 about a man who was paralyzed. His friends were sure Jesus could heal him, so they took him to the house where Jesus was. When they arrived, the house was packed with others who wanted to see Jesus. So what did they do? Give up? Say, "Sorry, buddy, maybe next time"? No, they found another way. They went up on the roof, made a hole, and lowered their friend into the room to Jesus.

When Jesus saw *their* faith, He healed the man on the mat. What a powerful picture of what having faith-filled friends can do. It can lead us to Jesus, to healing, and to finding our true purpose. Are your friends full of faith like that? Are your friends doing whatever it takes to bring you before Jesus? To get you healed? There will be moments in life you don't have the necessary faith on your own. There will be moments in your life you don't feel like you have what it takes to get to Jesus on your own. We all need friends who will take us to Jesus in those times.

Faith-filled friendships are necessary for healing. Scripture says in James 5 that when we confess to our friends and they pray for us, that's where we can be healed. We weren't made to live in isolation and secrecy. It's when we live in the light and invite people into our sin struggles and pain problems that we experience true healing. Like we have talked about before, healing requires revealing.

Remember when I shared earlier about my sin struggle

with pornography and masturbation? It wasn't until I confessed it to friends and they prayed for me that I truly experienced healing.

Faith-filled friendships are needed for everyday freedom. We can't trust ourselves alone. We all need accountability. Godly friendships aren't just for you to cry to and run to when you fall short. They are also meant to hold you accountable so that you don't fall. The right kind of friends help you cultivate guardrails and disciplines in your life so that you can live holy, set-apart lives for Jesus. Friends of faith help us be proactive, not just reactive, when it comes to sin. Not only did my friends pray with me when I confessed my struggle with sexual sin, they also helped me put a plan in place so that I could break free from that sin struggle.

> Friends of faith help us be proactive,
> not just reactive, when it comes to sin.

Faith-filled friendships help you defeat darkness. None of us can defeat darkness apart from the Holy Spirit. So that's a pretty essential ingredient. But we see throughout Scripture the importance of friendship when it comes to strengthening our faith.

In 1 Peter 5:8, we see that we all have an enemy who is after us: "Your enemy the devil prowls around like a roaring lion looking for someone to devour." Something I want to note here is that it says some*one*. Not a group of people. But one singular person. The enemy knows you are more likely to believe his lies and fall for his traps when you are all alone. We are more likely to fall into sin and believe lies when we are alone. But the right community helps us fight the enemy.

Faith-filled friendships help you love Jesus and accomplish His will for your life. The right friends not only help you fight off sin and Satan but will also push you to love Jesus with all your heart. They will encourage you with Scripture and pray for you and with you. It has brought so much joy to my life having friends who help me resist the bad and push me to God. We know that every good and perfect gift comes from God, and friendship is one of those gifts. When I am with my "God girls," I feel deep joy, peace, freedom, love, and contentment. Friendship isn't always easy, but it is so worth it.

So how do we find faith friends? And how do we cultivate those friendships?

FIND YOUR PEOPLE

While most of us desire deep and meaningful relationships, we often settle for less. Or we stay isolated. Let's address some ways that we *can* find and build those godly relationships that we deeply desire.

1. Pray for godly relationships.

We have talked about prayer a lot in this book. That's because it's powerful and important. I was taught growing up to "pray first." So when desiring to find your people, start by asking God to bring you those godly friends. In each season of my life—in moves, in transitions, in marriage, and now in parenting—I have prayed for godly community. That doesn't mean God is going to just deliver community to my door like my Amazon packages. I still have a role and responsibility on my end to build it. But prayer is the first step. Many of my friendships started in an "only God" kind of way, where I crossed paths with people in the most unexpected places. Pray that God would allow you to cross paths with someone or a group of people who can push you in your faith and help you love Jesus more.

2. Look in the right environments for the right friends.

Too many of us are looking in the wrong places for the right things. You aren't going to find your God-fearing bestie in the bar. Plug into a local church and small group. That is where I have met 90 percent of my closest friends. When Grant and I moved to Waco, Texas, we were newly married with no local friends. After joining a small group at our church, we began to find the friends we had been praying for. Now, living in Nashville, Tennessee, and having to start over with finding new friends, Grant and I have gotten plugged into a local church. We have joined a community group and the serve team. As much as we should pray in faith, we should also take steps of faith. Faith has footsteps. I know it can be scary to put yourself out there, especially when you are single. I remember when I was single and trying to find friends and I went to a small group by myself. I felt awkward and nervous. I even thought about leaving because I felt so anxious. But I stayed in it and kept going. And because of that, I met some of my best friends who ended up in my wedding. Making the first move and taking those steps of faith can be scary. Pray that God would give you strength, and then push yourself—it's so worth it!

3. Stop settling for *less* when you were made for *best*.

A lot of us treat our relationships and friendships like *Fixer Upper*. We think we can "save them." With a few renovations and conversations, they will be the person we want and need! But the Bible is clear that we should find friends that are like "iron" and our friendships should be like "iron sharpening iron"—strong, steady, and secure (Proverbs 27:17). That means both we and our friends have to be iron. We both have to be strong in our faith, all in, and committed to Jesus. The only way to find your iron is to let go of the wood or glass you have been settling for.

4. Be the kind of friend you want to have.

Don't wait for friends to find you. *You* step out, *you* invite, *you* be the encouraging one. A lot of times we wait around for others to pursue us, find us, and invite us. But that isn't how life works or even who God calls us to be. Instead of looking for what we can get, we should be looking for what we can give. Instead of wanting to be served, we should find ways to serve. We are to be the friend we are looking for. Do you want generous, honest friends, strong in their relationship with the Lord? Work on being those things. You'll attract who you are.

5. Put in the work.

When you are doing close life with people, moments will come when the relationship has conflict and tension. When that happens make sure you don't react out of anger or insecurity, but rather respond with grace and truth.

When conflict arises, the first thing to do is take it to God in prayer. Then evaluate yourself and see if there is something in you that needs to change. In these times, I always ask myself, "Is this a *me* problem?" Next, rather than complaining to someone else, go to the person to discuss the conflict, as Matthew 18:15 tells us: "Go and point out their fault, just between the two of you." You can ruin a friendship by gossiping to other people. Not to mention, gossip is a sin. If there is anything you need to own, own it. Own your part, even if it's 2 percent. Ask for forgiveness if you need to. Forgive them if you need to. And then move on. Life is too short to carry bitterness and unforgiveness and live offended. As humans, we will inevitably offend and disappoint each other.

Having godly friends will make you and your life better. True godly community holds you accountable and calls you higher, carries you when you are weak, helps you fight off sin and Satan, and pushes you closer to Jesus. Building godly community is a choice and will take effort, but it is worth it. Just like anything worthwhile, it's not going to happen accidentally. In order to stay true in this world, we have to have our people. So I dare you to find friends of faith!

DARE TO DO

Join a small group or Bible study at your local church.

12

DARE TO LIVE ON PURPOSE

Have you ever pooped your pants?

I have.

It happened in tenth grade. I had been asked by the headmaster of my school to share my testimony in front of the entire student body. I said yes right away because I knew I was supposed to do it. But then it hit me: I was going to be speaking to my peers, and even those way older than me. I was going to have the entire senior class sitting in chairs right in front of me. What those people thought of me mattered to me. Too much, really. The questions popped up in my head: *Who am I to share my testimony? Maybe someone else should do it. What if I say something dumb? Will they boo me offstage? Will they fall asleep?*

I prepared as best I could, and before I knew it the day arrived. So many questions and thoughts swam around in my head. As I sat in class waiting for the assembly, I was so nervous, and I even felt shame creep up, like I was unworthy to share my story. My gut churned with nervous energy. Next thing I knew, in math class, I started to feel a little weird in my tummy. I knew something was off, so I stood up and excused myself. As soon as I got up, I knew what was going on. I ran down the hall trying to make it to the girl's restroom. I didn't make it. Right there in the hallway. I pooped my pants.

When I got into the bathroom, I locked the stall door and sighed with relief. Frantically, I texted my mom to ask her to bring me new underwear. Not my finest hour. But Mama Prew came through and I got all cleaned up before my big moment.

When I finally got up in front of everyone to share my testimony, the nerves and shame I had been feeling started to go away, and I began to feel a kind of joy and purpose I had never known. None of the questions or worries mattered. All that mattered was sharing about all God had done for me. Even though I was still learning what a personal relationship with Jesus looked like and how to break free from my own sin struggles, I knew there was power in being vulnerable and honest. In that moment, I felt deep down that I was doing what I'd been made to do.

Afterward, several people came up to me and said that my words had a big impact on them and had challenged and inspired their faith walk. My sharing took courage, but it taught me something: *I was made for this.* I was made to share my story. I was made to point people to Jesus.

That day wasn't a win because of the humiliation of the morning or even the freedom of the afternoon when it was all over. It was a win because God had made me and prepared me for that moment. He made me to testify to His truth and to share how He was changing my life. When I was aligned with Him—even when living out my purpose cost me comfort—I was my most alive and free self. My life verse ever since has been Acts 20:24: "I consider my life worth nothing to me; my only aim is to finish the race and complete the task the Lord Jesus has given me—the task of testifying to the good news of God's grace."

The enemy has kept many of us from walking in our true God-given purpose. He has deceived many to believe that our purpose is about us and that we can find true fulfillment in this world. The mindset of our world today is "I only have energy for what serves me." We have confused purpose for platform and worldly success.

But like we talked about in previous chapters, the enemy is a liar! And the truth is that your purpose isn't about you. And my purpose isn't about me. It's so much bigger than us. We are part of a bigger picture, but we are not the picture. The picture is Jesus. He is the beginning, the right now, and the forevermore. We are like a breath, going away as quickly as it comes. This life is not all about us, and there is actually great hope and joy in understanding that. That perspective changed my life. And I have learned, even if walking in my true purpose comes with nerves, even if I am terrified to obey, if it glorifies God and I get to point to Him, I'm in!

> We are part of a bigger picture, but we are
> not the picture. The picture is Jesus.

Do you want to live a life of significance? Do you want your life to matter? Then it's time for you to discover what true purpose is and how you can find yours and live out exactly what He called *you* to do!

RUNNING WITH THE HORSES

Have you ever watched horse racing before? I will be honest, until I met my husband, I had never watched a horse race aside from when I was twelve years old and watched the movie *Spirit*. My husband and his family are big into horse racing. So I had to learn fast. While watching one of my first-ever horse races, I noticed something interesting that I had to ask Grant about. The horses raced with masks on. I asked Grant why, and he explained, "Those are called blinders. They keep the horse on track to run their race without distraction." The blinders were attached to the bridle and would cover the sides of the horse's eyes so they could only see what was right in front of them. Who knew horse racing was so inspiring!

So many thoughts flooded my mind as I watched these horses race with all their might. *Focus on what is in front of you. Run your race. Keep your eyes on the prize.* I was reminded that we too must run with determination and vision. That is our calling. That is what living our purpose should look like. But so often it's not.

A lot can get in the way of our purpose. I want to share the biggest hindrances I have seen in my own life and in those around me. We know that there are lies that often bind us and hold us back. Even when we know the truth that defeats the lie, we must continue in the truth and live it out so those obstacles don't keep us from our purpose. One of the biggest obstacles we have to overcome is *comparison*. So often we don't run our race because we are so consumed with everyone else's. We don't embrace our wiring and gifting because we are so focused on everyone else's. We get distracted from our calling as we are filled with jealousy and insecurity. The reason the horses had blinders on was to keep them from getting distracted by the other horses. They needed to see only what was right in front of them. They needed to stay in their lane and run their race. I think we could learn some things from horse racing. Many of us need to put on spiritual blinders, reminding ourselves of the truth about who God says we are and focusing on the race He has called us to run.

Another hindrance to our God-given purpose is *fear*. Fear can mask itself in many ways, whether that is insecurity because we feel unworthy, shame because we haven't resolved and healed from our past, or fear of failure. We convince ourselves it may be better not to try at all. Fear has a way of keeping us paralyzed or sidelined, where we miss out on everything God has for us. The enemy loves to use fear against us. He puts all these anxious and fearful thoughts in our minds. That's why phrases like "do not be afraid" and "do not worry" are repeated dozens of times in the Bible. I don't think that is coincidence. I believe that is because Jesus knew we would need new reminders every day to not let fear keep us from what God has for us.

Another hurdle to overcome when it comes to our purpose is *busyness*. The enemy will use distraction and activity to keep us from our purpose. Often we can't distinguish the difference between being busy and being purposeful. But let me be clear: Busyness does not equal productivity, nor does it equal purpose. We cannot let urgent things replace or distract us from important things. Many of us find that our lives are being defined by what's right in front of us rather than what matters most. True purpose requires us to value what is worthy over what is immediate.

> True purpose requires us to value what is
> worthy over what is immediate.

Sometimes the greatest obstacle we face is taking our eyes off the prize. Our goal—the prize, the ultimate reward—is why we run. And if we lose our why, we will lose our way. We will be aimless, like paper in the wind, with no true direction.

To live out the truth and live free, we have to block out the distractions and hindrances. But now let's talk about how we can set a vision for our lives and run the race that has been marked out for us.

WHAT WAS I MADE FOR?

We all have a deep desire to know why we were made and why on earth we are here. Without purpose, life feels pointless. Even if you chase all the things of this world and live in luxury and comfort, if you have no real purpose, you feel dead inside. That's because we were made *on* purpose and *for* a purpose.

It took me a while to discover my purpose, and even now

my purpose is continually unfolding. After I graduated college, I had no idea what I wanted to do. I had a ministry degree and a communications degree. My first job was in foster care and adoption. Although I am extremely passionate about it, the job was hard. It meant long hours, low pay, and being lonely. I worked from home and sat behind a computer. I knew it wouldn't be my job forever, but I tried to stay faithful.

After that job, I went on *The Bachelor.* (That took a weird turn, huh?) Yeah, well, it was a weird time. After I came off reality TV, I started doing social media. I didn't like that either. Then, about a year later, I got the opportunity to write my first book and speak. At first, I wasn't good at it. I had no idea what I was doing. I tried to speak and write like the people I looked up to. But then I didn't feel like myself, and I was miserable trying to be like other people. Over time, I learned how to develop my own voice and embrace the gifts God had given me.

One of my favorite verses that I would turn to when I questioned my purpose on this earth was Ephesians 2:10, which says, "For we are God's handiwork, created in Christ Jesus to do good works, which God prepared in advance for us to do." That means God had something for you and me to do before He even created us! He gave you your particular giftings and wiring for a special purpose.

Notice the order implied in that verse: God created a purpose for you, and *then* He created you for that purpose. It's what you were made for. That means that nothing about you is accidental, but rather it is all intentional. And that purpose drives your life. It's more than a platform and more than a status. It's your *why.* It's the reason behind everything you do.

Even Jesus had a unique, one-of-a-kind purpose. In Luke 19:10, Jesus says His purpose is "to seek and to save the lost." And in a conversation recorded in John 18 that led to Jesus being executed, He says this to Pilate when asked about His purpose, "In fact, the reason I was born and came into the world is to testify to the truth. Everyone on the side of truth listens to me" (verse 37). Jesus knew exactly what His purpose was.

In the same way, you and I have a purpose on this earth—a specific, unique, God-given purpose. In Paul's letter to the Romans we learn that we have all been entrusted with different gifts, but it's all to serve the same purpose: to edify others and glorify Christ! Romans 12:4–8 says:

> For just as each of us has one body with many members, and these members do not all have the same function, so in Christ we, though many, form one body, and each member belongs to all the others. We have different gifts, according to the grace given to each of us. If your gift is prophesying, then prophesy in accordance with your faith; if it is serving, then serve; if it is teaching, then teach; if it is to encourage, then give encouragement; if it is giving, then give generously; if it is to lead, do it diligently; if it is to show mercy, do it cheerfully.

So although we are made uniquely and intentionally, we are all a part of the same body—meaning we are not in competition with one another. We are not trying to outshine one another. The hand doesn't try to outdo the leg, or the toes the kneecap. And they definitely don't try to shine independently of each other. The hand doesn't decide to detach itself from the body so that it can have all the attention and glory. The toes don't decide to part ways and detach from the body because they want it to be more about them. No, they all work in tandem for the same purpose: to glorify God.

Your gift is special, but it is not meant to be selfish, but to serve. Your gifts are given for service. Your God-given, unique purpose was made for you, but it's not *meant* for you. Yes, God designed you for a special purpose, and that purpose is for God and to fulfill His work.

> Your God-given, unique purpose was made for you,
> but it's not *meant* for you.

In the same way, Jesus's purpose was not to inspire, make people happy, sit in a palace, or chill on the lake with some friends. He came to save. He came to set the captive free. He came to give His life as a ransom for many.

In the same way, you have been born for such a time as this, to use the gifts you have been given and the story that you have to serve others and glorify God.

THE GOOD GIFT-GIVER

My parents are the best celebrators. When I was little, they would put on special festivities to make me feel loved and valued. I can remember being so excited to get plastic Easter eggs filled with chocolates or plastic Barbie shoes, and lip balm for

Christmas. I was so grateful and appreciative because these gifts were given freely and in love.

As I grew older, I started to take those gifts for granted and wanted more for my own selfish purposes. As my middle school and high school friends received lots of luxury gifts like designer bags and jackets, my expectations for the same grew. I had outsized views on what I "deserved" and even started to demand certain gifts. It became all about me. My perspective shifted from gratitude to criticism, and my goal was to see how much I could get. Whenever I got a gift from my parents that wasn't what I wanted, I would throw a hissy fit. I would shut down, get upset, and isolate in my room like a brat. I look back now and see I was pretty entitled and pretentious. Thankfully I've grown out of that.

In the same way, many of us do this with the gifts God has given us. We throw a fit because it isn't what we want, or it isn't like *hers,* or it isn't what is seen as important or popular. So we get upset with God and we waste our time complaining and comparing instead of embracing our gifts by using them to serve others and glorify God.

I will be the first to admit that I struggle with this. Not just the bratty fits I threw when I didn't get what I wanted at Christmas, but the way I grumbled and complained about how I was wired: strong-willed, stubborn, and with a spirit that was unwilling to back down. I felt like my wiring constantly got me in trouble and made relationships hard. Girls didn't know how to be my friend, and guys didn't know what to do with me. I was viewed as "too much." For a long time I felt like I had to change myself to be liked.

Maybe you're in a season where you feel like this isn't where you want to be, you don't understand why you are where you are, and it feels hard. You know there is more for your life. Perhaps you are working a job right now that you don't like and is not what you feel called to do, but you have to make money. Maybe you struggle with how God wired you and the gifts He put inside of you, and you wish He would have given you different ones. Maybe you feel like the people around you don't appreciate or even see your gifts, and you feel helpless to know how to use them for good. You aren't alone. I have been there.

My encouragement to you is this: Don't desire the gifts more than the Giver. This is what the Holy Spirit had to correct in my heart. Not just as a bratty kid but also as an adult. I had to learn not to desire what God could give me or do for me, but rather learn to make Him my greatest desire. We quote verses like Psalm 37:4 and get them tatted on our bodies: "Delight in the LORD, and he will give you the desires of your heart." We think this verse means that because we follow God, He will give us whatever we want. But that is not what the verse is saying at all. Instead, it means that when we make God our everything, He is everything we want. He becomes our greatest desire. And His desires become our desires.

> When we make God our everything,
> He is everything we want.

My whole mindset toward my purpose changed when I stopped trying to use God to get what I wanted and instead learned to love God with all my heart—to make Him everything my heart wanted. Then I stopped hating how I was wired, stopped complaining about the season of life I was in, and stopped trying to walk in others' purposes.

I want you to know, no matter what lies the enemy has told you or what other people have spoken over you, God did not mess up with you. He has a plan and purpose for your life that are unique to you, because He loves you. And He has given you special and unique gifts not to bury them or run from them or use them for worldly, selfish gain, but to use them to bring Him glory.

THESE BOOTS ARE MADE FOR WALKIN'

Do you remember the song "These Boots Are Made for Walkin'"? I apologize for bringing up that song because now it will be stuck in your head. And just like boots are made for walking, and chairs are made for sitting, you are made for something—something great! You were made *on* purpose and *for* a purpose.

These are the steps I have found helpful for discovering true purpose in this life:

1. Discover your gifts.

We have talked a lot about gifts. Maybe you've thought, *But Madi . . . what* is *my gift?* Let's discover it! I discovered my gifts by trying new things and seeing what stuck and what I was good at. I also took lots of spiritual gift tests and personality assessments, and I prayed to God, asking Him to reveal my gifts to me. I also asked other trusted people what they saw in me. My gifts were revealed when I turned to prayer, meditating on Scripture, and asking godly community around me.

Not all gifts are alike, and just because someone you look up to or want to be like has a specific gift doesn't mean that is also your gifting. Often people come up to me and tell me they want to be in ministry and ask me for my advice and tips. But I always respond the same way: "Ministry is wherever your feet are." Ministry isn't about a microphone or teaching the Bible to a group of people or starting a podcast. Many want that to be their gifting because it gets people's eyes on them, but we have to remember that in order to be truly free, our purpose and giftings are not for selfish ambition or vain conceit, but rather for the glory of God.

Ask yourself, *What am I good at? What am I passionate about? What do other people affirm in me? What can I give to bless others? What does God's Word say about my purpose? When I pray about what I am called to do, what does God speak to me?* Now take some time to pray and journal about what you hear from God, your godly friends, and the Word of God.

2. Develop your gift.

Your gift will be developed over time. It may not look a whole lot like a gift right at the beginning, but it may grow the more you use it. For me, my speaking and writing has changed the more I do it. The more I practice, the more comfortable and confident I become. I push myself by creating challenging scenarios that grow my gift to communicate, such as giving myself tight timelines, putting myself on the spot in moments of pressure, or putting myself in uncomfortable or unfamiliar environments. The first time I spoke at a university and wasn't allowed to talk about my faith or include Scripture, I left feeling so defeated that I wanted to give up on speaking altogether. But really, that moment challenged me and grew my creativity.

Just like in sports, it takes practice to develop your skills before you feel fully confident and prepared for the big moments. The more you practice your gift, the more comfortable you will be using it.

I also would encourage you to find someone who has your same gifting but is a step ahead of you. Maybe that means finding a teacher with years of experience, a singer who has been leading others and traveling all over, or a writer whose words inspire you deeply. Or maybe it's a mom who has raised God-fearing children, a mentor who has led small groups effectively, or a friend who knows the Word of God and has Scripture memorized incredibly well. Find someone who is a few steps ahead of you and learn from them.

3. Dedicate your gifts to God and others.

God gave you gifts. But what you do with them is your gift back to God. You can't walk out your true purpose by using your gifts for selfish purposes or hiding them, but rather by using them to point back to Him.

And the greatest news ever is that when you are walking in

the purpose God made you for, He is the one leading you and sustaining you. He doesn't just leave it up to you to figure it out and make it happen. He is with you every step of the way. In Matthew 28:19–20, right before Jesus ascended to heaven, He gave this final commission to His disciples: "Therefore go and make disciples of all nations, baptizing them in the name of the Father and of the Son and of the Holy Spirit, and teaching them to obey everything I have commanded you. And surely I am with you always, to the very end of the age."

Notice two things here. First, your purpose will always be bigger than you. *Disciples of all nations?* That probably felt overwhelming for eleven men to hear. Similarly, your purpose will always feel too big for you—because it is. It's impossible for you, but possible with God.

Second, notice that God's presence is connected to our purpose. He says, "Go," but then follows it with, "I am with you." *You are not alone, and it is not up to you. Your purpose is from God, for God, and can only be accomplished through God.* He is the Giver and the Upholder. He is the Maker and the Sustainer. He is with us every step of the way as we walk out His purpose for our lives.

God's presence is connected to our purpose.

In the next chapter we are going to talk about how we can use our purpose to influence the world around us—for the glory of God!

DARE TO DO

Write out your own purpose statement or life verse.

Put it on your mirror or frame it to display.

Say it out loud daily.

13

DARE TO LIVE DIFFERENTLY

Spit was flying. Coach was in my face, shouting. Everyone was staring.

As I've mentioned, basketball was a huge part of my life, especially in high school when my dad was my basketball coach. He's the best coach I know, and I don't just say that because he's my dad. He doesn't just win games; he makes people winners in life. And it doesn't hurt that he's won over twenty-one championships in his thirty years of coaching.

Even though I enjoyed playing for my dad, having him yell at me was not my favorite.

I remember one game where we were down by double digits. It was starting to look like we would lose—something we rarely did. The only person I know who hates losing more than me is my dad. We should have been winning. We were the better team—even the most cynical person in the room would have told you that. But our team chemistry was off, and we had a new girl on the team who kept running the wrong plays, and it was costing us the game.

Coach (Dad) was doing his coaching thing, telling us where we could adjust so that maybe, just maybe, we could claw our way back to the top. But he didn't really direct that to the whole team—more just to me. And it wasn't in a suggestive, kind way; it was in a "PICK IT UP OR SIT THE BENCH!" kind of way. I felt angry and defensive. It wasn't my fault that one player on our team didn't know the plays. Why was he mad at me?

Usually I just said, "Yes, sir," and did what he asked of me. But this time I snapped. I defended myself at top volume, in front of the team and the whole crowd, yelling, "It's not my fault! Stop pointing fingers at me!"

My dad is the kind of guy who you do *not* talk back to. Ever. On the court or off the court. It was, like, his number one rule. He got nose to nose with me, veins popping out of his neck and spit flying, and he said something to me I'll never forget. He said, "You're the point guard, Madi. You're the leader of this team! And everything rises or falls on leadership!" Then he benched me.

That comment has stuck with me. I didn't like it in the moment, but he was right.

Of course, I didn't let him know that I knew he was right. Instead, I decided to be petty and prove a point. I sat on the end of the bench like I was happy to be there. I looked across at him and said, "Good luck winning without your point guard!" Yeah, not my best moment. We did end up losing the game, and everyone was discouraged. Later that night, I apologized to him and owned my part. He accepted my apology and reminded me in that moment the importance of leadership. He told me that he saw greatness in me and that he wasn't pushing me hard to humiliate me but to help me.

Now I am so grateful that I had someone see leadership potential in me, call it out of me, and help me walk in it. We all have that leadership potential. Sadly, many of us just don't like the cost that comes with it.

It is true that everything rises and falls on leadership. Who you are today and the person you are becoming has been influenced by leaders in your life, for better or worse. And in the same way, you are leading others, whether you realize it or not, in your action or inaction, in your words or silence, in your presence or withdrawal, in your joy or anger, in your positive and uplifting spirit or your negative and complaining attitude. You are influencing those in your life for bad or good. The simplest definition of leadership is influence. Anyone today can have followers, but it is what we are leading our followers toward that speaks to our true leadership.

> Anyone today can have followers, but it is what we are leading our followers toward that speaks to our true leadership.

Are you using your influence for good? Are you setting the tone, or are you letting the tone be set for you? Coach used to ask, "Are you a thermometer or are you a thermostat?" A thermometer will tell you the temperature but do nothing about it. All a thermometer does is assess. A thermostat, however, isn't passive—it's active. It reads the temperature as ninety-six degrees and blasts cold air so that the temperature can be cooler. The environment is improved. We're all happier we have thermostats around.

So let me ask you: Are you more like a thermometer, or are you a thermostat? Do you set the temperature, or do you let the temperature set you?

You were made to be a thermostat. *You* were made to lead. And in this chapter, we will talk about what true greatness and real, godly leadership looks like.

"WHEN I GROW UP, I WANT TO BE JUST LIKE YOU!"

Have you ever said the words, "I want to be just like _____ when I grow up"? I have. Maybe there's been someone in your life who stands out where you remember thinking, *What a leader!* Maybe it was a coach, a friend, a parent, a pastor, or someone you looked up to from afar. I have had a few people like that throughout my life. One girl who was a few grades above me, a senior in high school while I was a freshman, made every person she met better. She was my role model. She was unashamed of her love for Jesus and of her values. Some people picked on her and made fun of her because she didn't cuss, drink, listen to rowdy music, dance all wild, dress "sexy," and she had never kissed a boy. I remember thinking, *Is she an angel?*

She would lead our devotions before practice and games, would always be blaring worship music, encouraging others, serving, talking to someone left out, and singing joyfully (she had a beautiful voice).

I remember thinking, *She really doesn't care what other people think. She is unashamedly who God called her to be. She knows her mission in this life. She calls people higher—not just with her words, but also with the way she lives.*

I wanted to be just like her! I wrote her a letter telling her I wanted to be her when I grew up. She influenced me for the better. She made me want to love Jesus more. She made me want to serve and love on people. She made me want to be excellent in my sport and my schooling. She made me want to value my body and not give it away to anyone who would give it attention. There are leaders who come to mind who, throughout my life, have made a strong and positive impact on me, who have set an example that I wanted to follow. Can you think of someone who has done that for you?

Although we should find respectable, admirable leaders to look up to and learn from, there is only one leader we should fully follow. His name is Jesus.

In the Gospels, we see Jesus model true leadership. He was the only human being to ever live a perfect life. And His life, death, and resurrection changed our eternity and our relationship with God forever.

In Jesus's day, people expected the promised Messiah to ride in on a stallion with an army, a bodyguard, and a gold crown on his head. Everyone thought his leadership would be one of control, power, and status. Yet, Jesus was born from a virgin in a manger, lived in Galilee, and was a carpenter. After starting His public ministry, He chose disciples who were "nobodies" and sinners. The crown He wore was made of thorns, not gold. Not exactly what they expected for the Messiah, the One who would rewrite history and save the world, the greatest leader of all time.

But Jesus shows us what *true* greatness is and what real leadership looks like. He not only taught it, He lived it. In Matthew 20:25–28 Jesus tells His disciples (and us today) how to be a great leader like Him. He says,

> You know that the rulers of the Gentiles lord it over them, and their high officials exercise authority over them. Not so with you. Instead, whoever wants to become great among you must be your servant, and whoever wants to be first must be your slave—just as the Son of Man did not come to be served, but to serve, and to give his life as a ransom for many.

Jesus had every reason to sit back, let others feed Him grapes, set up a green room for Him with a feast, and tend to His every need. Yet He didn't choose that way. Instead, He served and laid His life down so that others may find life in Him. Even on the night when He knew He was going to be betrayed, Jesus put a towel around His waist, knelt, and washed His disciples' feet. This was the evening before Jesus would be crucified. His last hours with His boys would have been the perfect time to do an affirmation circle and have them all affirm Him. Or do a little gift exchange. Or even a time for Jesus to rest and prepare for the arduous night ahead and let them serve Him. Yet, Jesus did not think of Himself.

He thought about His disciples. This was an extreme act of servanthood.

Poignantly, the disciples had just been debating who was the "greatest" and what greatness looked like. But Jesus illustrated true greatness. It was customary that the lowest servant of the house would wash the feet of the guests as they came into the house, especially for a formal meal like this. Think about how gross their feet would have been after traveling all day on dirt roads in sandals. But here was Jesus, the Son of God with all power and authority, taking a towel and washing His disciples' feet.

He then taught His disciples that they should also wash one another's feet. This wasn't just for them in that moment in time; it is metaphorically true for you and me and every follower of Jesus Christ. Not necessarily that we walk around with buckets and towels, asking people to take off their shoes. But that we should always choose to go low, consider others as more important than ourselves, and serve out of humility and love. If you want to lead on the highest level, be willing to serve on the lowest.

> If you want to lead on the highest level,
> be willing to serve on the lowest.

Jesus, the greatest leader of all time, the real GOAT, showed us that leadership is not holding the microphone, reigning over people, having the blue checkmark, or getting a successful business deal. It's service. And Jesus didn't just tell us, "Hey, go serve." He served. He didn't just say, "Lay your life down for others," He laid His life down for us. He led so we can follow and do as He did. And as we follow Him, we lead others to Him.

THE INFLUENCER ~~TREND~~ TRAP

"I want to be an influencer" is a statement that people say a lot today. Even though we are all called to influence, many of us have a wrong view of what real influence is. We confuse it with status, power, and social media followers. That's because the devil knows that servant leadership advances God's kingdom and reign, so he will do anything to corrupt and deceive us into thinking that prideful and selfish leadership is better. And he's done a pretty good job by sneakily advancing ideas about what leadership looks like. You can spot this worldly leadership because it's all about self. The world's way of "influencing" is not service oriented, nor is it to glorify God. It's all about getting glory for self.

Sadly, I even see this self-focused leadership in the Christian "influencer" and "famous pastor" space. But this is not what God desires or what God calls true influence. This fake influence keeps us from having real influence. Jesus also rebukes false leadership and warns us against the kind of leaders we shouldn't listen to or become. Matthew 23:2–12 says:

> The teachers of the law and the Pharisees sit in Moses' seat. So you must be careful to do everything they tell you. But do not do what they do, for they do not practice what

they preach. They tie up heavy, cumbersome loads and put them on other people's shoulders, but they themselves are not willing to lift a finger to move them. *Everything they do is done for people to see:* They make their phylacteries wide and the tassels on their garments long; they love the place of honor at banquets and the most important seats in the synagogues; they love to be greeted with respect in the marketplaces and to be called "Rabbi" by others. But you are not to be called "Rabbi," for you have one Teacher, and you are all brothers. And do not call anyone on earth "father," for you have one Father, and he is in heaven. Nor are you to be called instructors, for you have one Instructor, the Messiah. The greatest among you will be your servant. For those who exalt themselves will be humbled, and those who humble themselves will be exalted.

Jesus rebuked the Pharisees because they sought public adoration instead of private dedication. They sought credit and attention for themselves instead of giving all glory to God. That's why we can't confuse status with leadership. We can't confuse platform and power with purpose. Influencers and others who have a large following but are leading their followers only for themselves are not true leaders, at least not leaders that please God. When we lift ourselves up for our own glory, God will humble us, and no true fruit will come out of any of it. But when we humble ourselves before God and let our lives be an offering to Him, He can use us for His purposes and His kingdom in great and mighty ways.

The enemy has deceived our world today with his lies

about what true leadership and influence looks like. He has sold our culture the lie that influence is about what you can get, how much you can make, and how many followers you have. He tells us that influence is all about power and status. But following the ways of the world and believing the lies of the enemy doesn't lead to freedom and contentment. We see that with the celebrities of today. *For those who have it all, if it's not all for God, it's all for nothing.* Because at the end of everything, what lasts? What can you take with you? Even if you gain the whole world, achieve every worldly dream you ever had, earn masses of social media followers, and make millions of dollars, at the end of your life it's you alone in a casket, and all your work will have been for nothing.

If I'm being honest, this is something I struggle with and have to give to God daily. I want people to like me. I want to feel important. I like what worldly success provides. And I have to die to those feelings every day and ask God to give me a spirit of humility and to help me steward everything He has given me for His glory. When I choose to make it all about me, I feel the weight of it—I'm overwhelmed, exhausted, and insecure, feeling like I can never do enough to keep up. But when I give God my purpose and influence others for Him, I feel free.

True leaders have eternal perspective, not oversized egos. They seek to exalt the name of Jesus, not their own name. True leaders have treasures that are everlasting, that won't spoil, fade, or get taken away. They know true leadership is service to the True Leader.

BECOMING A LEADER WORTH FOLLOWING

Maybe you don't feel much like a leader without any type of position or influence. Maybe you feel like, "Oh, Madi, this doesn't really apply to me." That's just not true. That is a lie the enemy wants you to believe. We are all leaders. We all have been called to lead. Whether or not you realize it, you are always influencing those around you. It doesn't matter how old you are or how many "followers" you have—the Word tells us we are to be set apart and we are to set an example for others.

So how can you be a leader worth following? Here are five ways:

1. Be led.

To lead well, you have to be led well. To be the leader God calls us to be, we need to make sure God is always the one in the driver's seat, leading us. It's impossible to give from an empty cup. And remember, we are told in John 15 that apart from Him we have nothing. But we are also told in Philippians 4 that we can do all things in His strength. It is important for us to understand that we have nothing to give others if we are not first being filled up by Him. In order to have any type of true impact and bear fruit that will last, we must be led by the True Leader. For me, I do not leave my house until I have spent time in God's presence and in His Word. I know that I have nothing to give in my own strength. The only way I can lead others to anything of true significance is if I first die to myself and let the Spirit of God fill me and lead me. In order to lead effectively, we must first be led intimately.

In order to lead effectively,
we must first be led intimately.

2. Lead yourself.

To lead others we must first lead ourselves well. Just like Jesus rebuked the Pharisees for teaching others truth yet not following it themselves, we must practice what we preach. Jesus modeled first what it looked like to serve before He called His followers to serve. Before telling His disciples to pray when under temptation and pressure, Jesus Himself prayed when He was overwhelmed. In the same way, we are to make sure we are leading ourselves well before we try to lead others. In order to be a great leader for others, we must first be a great leader of ourselves. For me that looks like having mentorship and accountability (because I can't do it alone and I have many blind spots), developing self-discipline (because desire without discipline is dead), abiding daily in the Word of God and prayer (filling myself with God's instruction), and living out what I read and talk about (practicing what I preach).

What are you doing to lead yourself well? How can you lead yourself better? What changes do you need to make?

3. Find ways to serve.

Jesus showed us that true leadership is true service. The greatest leaders are the greatest servants. To the world, "leadership" is power and platform, but to a true follower of Jesus, leadership is sacrifice and service. That means leaders don't walk into rooms and think, *Here I am.* Rather, they walk into rooms thinking, *There they are.* It's not about you, it's about others. And you can make it about others by serving them with the gifts God has given you, whether the gift of speaking, singing, playing an instrument, hospitality, encouragement, creativity, or any other gifts. Whatever your abilities are, use them for the glory of God and for the betterment of the people around you. We talked in the last chapter about how God has given us each different gifts and that those gifts aren't for ourselves. They are given to be offered back. This can feel confusing . . . *Didn't you give this to me, God?* But the truth is that when we use the gifts God has given us to serve others, we feel joy in a much greater way than when we use them for our own selfish gain. Ask yourself, *How well do I serve others?* and *Am I constantly looking for people to serve me, or am I looking for ways to serve other people?* Check your heart and motives, and then put service into action! There are ways to serve people every single day.

> To the world, "leadership" is power and platform,
> but to a true follower of Jesus, leadership
> is sacrifice and service.

4. Add value wherever you are.

True leaders add value everywhere they go, making rooms and the people in them better. They do this by finding a need and meeting it. Great leaders see problems and offer solutions. They don't just see a problem, they see the potential. They don't just talk about the problem, they fix it.

I remember when I interned for a pastor at a church one semester in college, and every week he would ask me for feedback on the Sunday service (usually I would have to type it out and send it to him via email). I would point out what was good, what needed to be improved, and where we were lacking as a church. The first few times I emailed him, he didn't give me a response. But one week, he challenged me: "So what is the solution?" I didn't know how to answer. He encouraged me that in being a leader worth following, I should always look for ways that things could be better, but then I should do something to improve the situation.

It's the idea of "If not you, then who?" So many of us wait around for other people to step up. But a real leader is always finding a way to raise the bar. When you walk into a room, think to yourself, *How can I leave this place better than I found it?* When you spend time with someone think, *How can I add value to their life?*

5. Be set apart.

In 1 Timothy 4:12 we are told that real leaders are set apart from the rest of the crowd and that they set an example for others. The verse says, "Don't let anyone look down on you because you are young, but set an example for the believers in speech, in conduct, in love, in faith and in purity." If we want to be people worth following, we are to be set apart in the words we say, the decisions and choices we make, the beliefs and perspectives we have, the love we show and give, and in the purity of our hearts and lives. True leaders don't look like the rest of the world. They don't just follow the crowd and do whatever is comfortable, easy, or popular. They follow God's standard of living, and they lead others to do the same.

The enemy and the world will try to keep you from all God has for you, keeping you stuck in the deceptive philosophy that many follow when it comes to real influence and leadership. But that is not what God has for you. God has *more* for you. You were born to lead.

In the final chapter we will talk about how not to return to the bondage of our pasts and instead live in freedom every day. It's time to dare to be free!

DARE TO DO

Find a serve project through your church or in your community, and invite your friends to join you!

14

DARE TO LIVE FREE

Recently I saw a video on social media of a man saving a sheep.

This sheep was stuck in a dangerous crevice and couldn't get itself out. The man worked to rescue the sheep, then cheered it on to its freedom. Only, immediately after being rescued, the sheep ran right back into the crevice and got stuck again. The man shook his head and let out a sigh.

Isn't this often a picture of you and me? We return right back to what Jesus set us free from. We go back to that thing that kept us stuck and bound in the first place. Jesus, the great Rescuer, saves us. And how many times do we turn back to the trap of bondage rather than running to the field of freedom?

Galatians 5:1 says, "It is for freedom that Christ has set us free. Stand firm, then, and do not let yourselves be burdened again by a yoke of slavery." Paul was begging believers, "Don't go back to bondage, please. Don't go back to what bound you!"

We won't be perfect. We will fail and slip up again. And God's grace will be ready to meet us every single time. But my prayer for you and me is that though our faith may falter, may it not fail. Jesus prayed for Peter when Satan asked for permission to have him, and I believe it's the same prayer He prays for us. In Luke 22:31–32, Jesus said to Peter (also known as Simon), "Simon, Simon, Satan has asked to sift all of you as wheat. But I have prayed for you, Simon, that your faith may not fail. And when you have turned back, strengthen your brothers." Jesus prays that our faith will not fail. Even when it falters and falls short, may we have the courage to repent and keep going, not returning to who we once were.

The reality is that even if you have been set free and you know the truth, you still have to make the decision every single day to walk in that truth. In order to stay free, you have to make the choice every day to follow the real truth that leads to real freedom. You will have many moments when you could choose to follow the ways of the world and go back to the bondage of your past, but I dare you to choose freedom.

Have you ever heard the song "Shackles" by Mary Mary? "Take the shackles off my feet so I can dance!" That was *my* song growing up. I could sing every lyric to you right now.

The first time I heard it was at church camp. Each summer's week at church camp was always my favorite of the whole year. All throughout the week there would be worship, recreation, swimming, and crafts. But my favorite part of camp was the last night when everyone would perform the stage dramas they had been learning all week. My group (about eight other girls my age) decided to do our drama to "Shackles." We made shackle-like paper-chain links to go around our hands and feet. We practiced every day to prepare for the big moment.

When the night finally came, we lined up and made our way to the stage, walking slowly with our "bound" hands and feet. As we sang the first part of the song, we slowly moved around with our shackles, bound and limited in movement. When the chorus hit, and the line "Take the shackles off my feet so I can dance" came on, we jumped in sync, spreading our feet out and pulling our hands apart, sending the paper shackles flying. It was a powerful moment that showcased breaking free from sin and the weight that keeps us stuck.

I've been reminded of that moment so often while writing this book because that's a picture of all of us. We are either walking in shackles, stuck in sin, bound by weight . . . *or* we're living free, worshipping and singing, released through Christ. The shackles come off when we stop believing the lies of the world, falling for temptation, and living in sin. When we know the truth and walk in it, we're able to break free.

By now you know that we can't set ourselves free. Only the blood of Jesus can. Just like Grant and I needed that plumber to save us from the gas leak that was slowly killing us, just like my sister needed my dad to bail her out of the jail cell she got herself into but couldn't get herself out of, and just like the story of me almost drowning in the wave pool until the nice man reached under the water and rescued me, it takes some-one outside of you, greater than you, to save you. There is only One who can set us free, and only by Him and through Him can we stay free. His name is Jesus.

WRONG WAY, WRONG DESTINATION

My husband is the worst driver ever.

(Grant, if you are reading this, I'm sorry and I love you, but we both know it's true.)

Grant will hit curbs, miss exits, run red lights, and engage in full conversation with you, looking you in the eyes instead of looking at the road. I pray over his driving every day.

Back when we lived in Waco, Texas, any time we had an early flight, we would choose to stay with his parents who lived two hours away in Dallas, since the airport was only about fifteen minutes from their house. There was a night we needed to stay there because I had an early flight the next morning for a speaking engagement. The plan was to leave right when Grant finished work, but a really bad storm hit, which then turned into a tornado with golf-ball-sized hail (Texas weather). So we took cover and waited it out.

When the storm finally passed, it was after 10 P.M. We hit the road quickly, ready to get to Dallas and get some sleep. About halfway, I told Grant I needed to stop to use the bathroom, so he turned off the navigation and stopped at a gas station. When I got back in the car, he clicked back on his navigation, pressed "home," and hit the road again. We had about an hour left.

Because it was getting late and we were so tired, we decided to play games to stay awake. We ended up enjoying the drive and when the navigation said we were about twenty minutes from our destination . . . we started to notice some weird things—like the Baylor football stadium. *Wait, that stadium is in Waco—not Dallas!* We couldn't believe our eyes. *You mean to tell me that this whole time we've been driving was all for nothing?!* We realized that when Grant had hit the "home" button, Maps took him to our Waco home and not his parents' Dallas home.

So, at midnight, shocked and delirious, we decided to get a Sonic slushie, blare our favorite music, and drive back to Dallas. I told you he was a bad driver! But I guess you could say I am to blame for having a small bladder and then not noticing that we were headed in the completely opposite direction.

The whole time we were driving, we felt we were headed to the right destination. We were confident in our way. But we had a wake-up call. A realization that we were going the wrong way, and it cost us time and sleep. In the same way, there are many today going the wrong way, headed to the wrong destination, and it will cost them a lot more than sleep. Many follow "their truth" and the world's way of "freedom," but it's a way that leads to bondage and death.

The Bible says in 2 Peter 2:19, "They promise them freedom, while they themselves are slaves of depravity—for 'people are slaves to whatever has mastered them.'" So many of us are looking for the right thing in the wrong places. We all want to feel "alive" and "free," yet in following the world's way, we drive reckless and wild, with no true direction, and the road we are on leads to death. *The world's version of freedom is bondage.*

I saw this same pattern play out while I was watching the movie *The Chronicles of Narnia* the other day. The White Witch deceived one of the main characters, Edmund, by appealing to his desire for power and by feeding his appetite. This is the same play the devil runs on us. When Edmund fell for her trickery, he discovered he didn't receive what he thought he would. She promised him freedom and power, but all he got was chains, shame, and a cold prison cell. His wasn't a path that led to freedom; it was a path that led to bondage.

That's what the enemy does. The devil dangles diamonds, but then he traps you in torment. You think, *If I just get this or do this, then I will be happy.* And then when you get "the thing," whatever it is, you realize the hole in your heart still isn't filled. If anything, it's even bigger. And it often leads to a prison of shame and bondage. Because freedom isn't found in you. It isn't found in the world.

> The devil dangles diamonds,
> but then he traps you in torment.

God has a better way, a way of fulfillment and of life. But many are going the wrong way, down a road that leads to defeat, destruction, darkness, and death. Just like Proverbs 14:12 tells us, "There is a *way* that appears to be right, but in the end it leads to *death*." The world's way leads to death. But that's not the only verse that speaks to a way that leads to a destination. Jesus says in John 14:6, "I am *the way* and *the truth* and *the life*." His way leads to life. He is the way of truth. Every answer you are searching for about your purpose, identity, and eternity is found in Him. *God has a better way for you, and His path to truth and freedom is a path that leads to life.*

And if you're thinking, *I have been driving the wrong way! There is no hope for me, Madi,* the good news is, if you choose right now to accept Jesus into your heart and trust in Him, your *way* changes, which means your destination changes. That's what the word "repentance" literally means—to change directions. To repent is to turn *from* something *to* something. To stop going the wrong way, turn around and start going the right way. Jesus made the way for you. He became the way—the way to life everlasting. And that destination is a whole lot better!

Finding freedom in Jesus flips everything. Jesus gives us freedom from sin, spiritual bondage, and death. We have talked throughout this book about how there is a liar named Satan who comes after you, trying to sell you fake freedom.

But together we have learned how to break free from his lies and live out the truth—truth found in Jesus. Jesus doesn't offer us fake freedom that lasts for a second and then leads to a cold prison cell. His freedom gives us abundant life.

What a journey we have been on! But I must warn you as we come to the end of our time together, you still have quite the road ahead. And so do I. A road we will be on for as long as we are on this earth. There will be a temptation to go back—to go back to what once enslaved you. To go back to what kept you bound. And this is my warning and charge to you: Don't go back. It's not enough to just get free. Now it's time to *stay* free.

LIVING IN FREEDOM EVERY DAY

This reminds me of a time when I went to an escape room with my mom and sisters. Oh, man, my blood was pumping the whole time! I felt anxious—the pressure to figure out the way to freedom while the clock was ticking. And sadly, we didn't succeed. Why not? *We didn't ask for help.* We were told at the beginning that we would be given a guide, a helper. But we didn't lean on him or ask him for clues. We thought, *We've got this!* Then, with just minutes remaining, our thoughts changed to, *Oh, man, we made a mistake!*

Remember, you and I aren't meant to break out—to find freedom and stay free—all on our own. We were sent a Helper, the Holy Spirit, to guide us in our quest for truth and true freedom. The Holy Spirit, also called the Spirit of truth and the Helper, was sent to lead us to the path of life. Jesus says in John 16:13, "When he, the Spirit of truth, comes, he will guide you into all the truth." You can't find the truth or walk in the truth on your own, and neither can I. The only way we walk in freedom every day is by following the Spirit and letting Him guide us into the truth.

Scripture is clear—we can't find our own way, make our own way, or follow the ways of the world to real freedom. Jesus is the only way. Don't get me wrong—we have a responsibility on our end. We don't just sit back and let the Holy Spirit do all the work. We have to ask for help and then follow where the Spirit leads. Some of us don't ask for help (just like my sisters and me in the escape room), and some of us know the way but choose not to follow.

As we wrap up our journey together, I want to share with you three practices that allow me to walk in freedom every day, and I hope they empower you to do the same.

1. Recognize the lies and stay in the truth.

The only way we overcome the lies of the enemy is by knowing God's truth and replacing the lies with the truth. You may have a very real enemy, but even more importantly, you have a very real God, who holds all power. Ephesians 1:21 says Jesus is "far above all rule and authority and power and dominion, and above every name that is named, not only in this age but also in the one to come" (ESV). Although the lies often feel strong, the truth is stronger and can defeat all lies. But in order to rebuke Satan's lies, we have to know the Truth, which means we have to stay in the Word.

The Word of God isn't meant to be just a book or an app you open on your phone when you feel like it; it's meant to be written on your heart. The Word of God is not a cake to be consumed on special occasions. It's our daily bread that keeps us alive. We have to make God's Word a consistent priority.

The only way we have the Word written on our heart is if we spend time in it and meditate on it and memorize it. If you can remember the lyrics to your favorite songs or social media trends, you can commit passages from Scripture to memory. Start small with a verse each week. The memory is like a muscle. It gets stronger as you use it more.

Then apply the Word (Truth) to your life and let it lead to

action. James 1:22 says, "Do not merely listen to the word, and so deceive yourselves. Do what it says."

The only way I am able to walk in true freedom every day and overcome the lies that come my way is by using the Word of God as my weapon.

2. Pray and praise continually.

I know we had an entire chapter on prayer and have talked about it quite a lot, but prayer is not just important to get free; it's necessary to stay free. I want to re-emphasize that this is how I stay free every day. I stay "prayed up." I pray all throughout the day, and I have my people praying. When I feel under attack, weary, anxious, confused, or overwhelmed, I text a few of my close friends and ask them to pray. Every single night before Grant and I go to bed, we pray together. And any time we are making big decisions in life or have something heavy going on, we will fast and pray. Why? Because it works. Because it keeps us desperate for Jesus and connected to Him. And because it helps us fight our flesh, the temptations around us, and the lies that the enemy uses against us.

The enemy will do everything he can to keep us from praying and speaking the truth to defeat his lies. He will put discouragement, depression, distraction, busyness, or even success in our lives to keep us from being watchful and prayerful continuously. The devil knows that 2 Corinthians 10:4–5 is true: "The weapons we fight with are not the weapons of the world. On the contrary, they have divine power to demolish strongholds

[lies]. We demolish arguments and every pretension that sets itself up against the knowledge of God." When we pray, especially when we pray the Word of God, we defeat lies and tear down the enemy's strongholds.

I have made this a discipline in my life because I have learned that I can't afford not to pray. And not just for myself. I am called to pray for those around me. I pray for my spouse, my family, my country, my church, the lost, and those neglected. I have a prayer wall full of prayers I am believing God for.

Acts 16:25–26 says, "About midnight Paul and Silas were praying and singing hymns to God, and the other prisoners were listening to them. Suddenly there was such a violent earthquake that the foundations of the prison were shaken. At once all the prison doors flew open, and everyone's chains came loose." We see here that because of Paul and Silas's prayers of praise, not only were they set free, but those around them were saved and set free also. True prayer and praise bring freedom to our lives, *and* they have the power to bring freedom to others.

Your freedom isn't from you or for you. You have been set free to set other people free. And one of the greatest ways you do that is by prayer. Do you have a friend or family member who doesn't know Jesus? Do you have a severed and broken relationship that needs restoration? Do you have someone in your life who needs healing or a miracle? Pray. And praise God for who He is and what you believe He can and will do! We walk in freedom every day by praying continually.

3. Live for eternity.

One of the greatest ways we defeat our enemy and walk in true victory and freedom is by remembering that we are citizens of heaven, living for eternity. Although we can experience freedom in Christ here on this earth, there is an eternal freedom that is to come where there will never again be sadness, sin, separation from God, shame, or anything bad. We know that here on earth we will have to fight to keep our faith and freedom in Christ, knowing that one day there will be a reward and everlasting blessing. James 1:12 says, "Blessed is the one who perseveres under trial because, having stood the test, that person will receive the crown of life that the Lord has promised to those who love him." *True freedom isn't found in the immediate but in the ultimate, our true reward in heaven.* We run our race and stay in the truth for a crown that will last forever. We store up for ourselves treasures that will not rust or fade away. And whatever we face here, whatever troubles or tribulations may come, we press on in confidence and hope because there is an eternal glory promised to us that will far outweigh it all. We stay true now so that we can live free forever.

We stay true now so that we can live free forever.

STAY TRUE

This year I started a podcast called *Stay True*. I spent months praying over the name and ended up landing where I did because it rhymed with my nickname, Madi Prew. At the time, I didn't really know what I wanted the podcast to be about, but as I prayed about it, I knew I was called to speak and share truth. Ironically, I first had the idea about writing about truth three years before I actually started writing this book.

As I started writing and researching, I changed the topic and direction multiple times. I almost walked away from writing the book many times because of the spiritual warfare and writer's block I was feeling. I'll be honest, having your book published feels good. *Writing* the book feels anything but that. It's long, hard, and vulnerable, filled with lonely days, a sore back, and strained eyes, and many weights and warfare come with it. But I know if I press on and let *God do God*, the long, hard process could lead to someone else finding freedom.

Writing this book has been one of the most humbling, challenging, and convicting things I've ever done. Truth be told (no pun intended), I didn't feel qualified or good enough to write this book, because I have had moments where I haven't always "stayed true." So if that is how you feel reading it, know that even the one writing it has felt that way. And as I wrap up this book, I want to emphasize that you never arrive in "becoming true." It's a constant journey of refinement, purification, humility, and growth. I am constantly growing in my relationship with Jesus and knowledge of His Word and how to follow it with all my heart.

I know we have talked about a lot of stuff in this book, and if you are anything like me, you might suffer from short-term memory loss like Dory from *Finding Nemo*. It can be hard to know all the truths, and it can feel overwhelming to do all the dares. Take a deep breath. Remember that you can't do anything good apart from Him, but with Him, you can do all things.

And wherever you are in your journey of "daring to be true," you aren't alone. God doesn't want perfect performance. He just wants your heart. As you seek Him with everything you have, He begins to change you, give you a new heart with new desires, and equip you to live the life of purpose and truth He has called you to live.

In a world that is constantly throwing around ideas of what truth is, we must know the real Truth and stay true to Him. The world's truth is constantly changing. But the Truth is never changing. And the best part? He sets us *free*.

The freedom we find through Christ is freedom from having to earn our way to God. It's freedom from sin and guilt and condemnation. Freedom from the penalty and the power of sin. Freedom to be made new, to walk in our God-given purpose, and to experience life to the fullest, on earth and in heaven. That freedom is found when we know and believe the Truth.

Just like when Grant and I found out about the truth of our suffering—the gas leak—it would have been useless and crazy for us to have the plumber turn off the gas, only for us to turn it back on the next day. Maybe, as you've been reading this book, the Holy Spirit has been convicting you and you have identified the problem—what has been breaking you. Maybe now it is time to do something about it. Don't just let it stay a problem. Don't just settle for suffering and bondage. God has more for you. You might have made the decision to go all in with Jesus, and you finally feel free. My challenge for you is to keep walking in that freedom every day. It's not a one-time moment; it's an everyday decision.

There is nothing like the freedom we can have in Jesus. No money can buy it, no status can obtain it, no works can earn it, and nothing can match it.

Living free indeed is who you were made to be. Now I dare you to stay true!

ACKNOWLEDGMENTS

Grant: Thank you for reminding me of the truth when I forget, for praying truth over me when I have believed lies, and for living on mission to share the truth alongside me. Since being married to you, I have become more like Jesus and have experienced more of the abundant life Jesus promised His followers. Thank you for never letting me settle, for always encouraging me, and for leading this family in grace, humility, joy, and truth. You believe in me and support me. You read through this entire book and gave me feedback, and you have helped me press on through this writing journey when I wanted to quit many times. I thank God He gave me a spouse like you, and I am proud to be your wife. You inspire me every day to stay true and live free. I love you forever.

Hosanna Rose: Thank you for giving me the gift of motherhood. You have brought me more joy and purpose than I ever knew would be possible. I pray you know the Truth all the days of your life. And that you keep your childlike faith and live freely and fully who He has made you to be. I am honored to be your mom. You are so deeply loved—first by Him, and always by me! You will always be my little Hosie Rosie!

Dad and Mom: Thank you for teaching me the truth and training me in it. You are the world's best parents and had the beautiful balance of compassion and grace with discipline and truth. Because of the way you modeled in our home what it looks like to radically follow Jesus, I have known the Truth on a personal level since my youth. Mom, you spoke and sang Scripture over me, you reminded me of my true worth and identity in Christ, and you taught me how to give generously to those in need. Dad, you disciplined me in righteousness and taught me the importance of fearing God and staying true to His commands—and how to work hard with all that I do. I pray that Grant and I can be parents like you have been, full of faith, encouragement, love, and truth.

Mallory and Mary: Thank you for being the best sisters and friends a girl could ask for. You have both become mighty women of God and I am inspired and encouraged by your faith. Mallory, you have a heart for the hurting, the orphaned, and the poor, and it pleases God and inspires those around you. You find joy in the simple things of life, and I know that your childlike faith is what we should all strive to have. Mary, you have a heart to spread the gospel, go to the un-reached and bring freedom, and worship Jesus with all your heart, and it pleases God. Your zeal for the Lord and desire to be with Jesus and talk about Him all the time inspires those around you. I love you both with all my heart and love seeing you become the best aunts to our baby girl!

Meme and Mimi: Thank you both for being present, intentional, and loving grandmothers. Mimi, thank you for always praying for me, encouraging me with the Word, and modeling what it looks like to be a woman who fears the Lord. You have shown your family faithfulness in how you serve God and the people of God. Meme, thank you for always supporting me and believing in me, making memories and going on adventures with me, and your intentional and thoughtful letters and gifts I will cherish forever. I am grateful that I had godly grandmas, and I love you both more than you will ever know!

The Troutt family: Kenny, you have led fearlessly and generously. Thousands of lives have been impacted by you. And your smile is my favorite thing! Mama Lisa, you are a truth warrior! I love the way you fight for truth. And I am grateful for your love and encouragement always. Preston, you are a leader and carry a shameless spirit. You are undeniably yourself and I love that about you. Thank you for being an amazing brother and friend to Grant and for always making me feel seen and loved. Savannah, you carry yourself with so much grace. You have a beautiful heart to serve and love on those who get overlooked and forgotten, and I know that is the heart of our heavenly Father.

Brother Don and Sarah Davis: Thank you for teaching me what it looks like to be a true worshipper: worshipping God in spirit and in truth. Under your leadership at Atmore First Assembly, I encountered the living God for the first time and made a decision from a young age to follow Him. Camp AFA was where I got filled with the Holy Spirit and made memories I will never forget. I am grateful not only for the impact you both have had on my life directly, but also the way you have influenced my parents' lives. We will be forever grateful for you and your family!

Curtis and Karen Yates and the Yates and Yates team: Thank you for believing in me and for standing by my side through this book. There were many obstacles to overcome and many days this project felt overwhelming and exhausting. I am thankful for your patience and prayers and determination. It's an honor to be on mission with you!

The WaterBrook team: Thank you for your belief in this message and in me. Thank you for being wise, prayerful, and gracious with this book and with me! Y'all are the dream team and an answer to many prayers.

To all my other friends and family: Your love has carried me through and pushed me onward when I wanted to give up and quit. Your prayers have held me up when I was weak, your encouragement kept me going when I was doubtful, and your constant presence in my life has made me who I am today. I love you.

To you, my reader friends: When I felt like giving up on this book and message, I thought about you. With the lies you have believed, the weights you have carried, the confusion you have felt, I knew I had to write to you on the truth that not only saves, but sustains and sets free. I pray that as you read through this book you feel challenged and encouraged to confront lies, find and face the truth, follow that truth, and ultimately live the life you were made for—a life of true purpose and freedom.

ABOUT THE AUTHOR

MADISON PREWETT TROUTT is a speaker, social media influencer, host of the *Stay True* podcast, and bestselling author of *Made for This Moment* and *The Love Everybody Wants*. She has a degree in communications from Auburn University and a certificate in ministry in pastoral leadership through Highlands College.

Her life mission is to share the name of Jesus and to help people find the real truth that leads to real freedom.

Madison Prewett Troutt and her husband, Grant, live in Nashville, Tennessee, and enjoy spending their time being plugged into their local church, telling people about Jesus, serving their community, and loving on their new baby girl, Hosanna Rose.

ABOUT THE TYPE

This book was set in Baskerville, a typeface designed by John Baskerville (1706–75), an amateur printer and typefounder, and cut for him by John Handy in 1750. The type became popular again when the Lanston Monotype Corporation of London revived the classic roman face in 1923. The Mergenthaler Linotype Company in England and the United States cut a version of Baskerville in 1931, making it one of the most widely used typefaces today.

Also from bestselling author
MADISON PREWETT TROUTT

Madi knows what it's like to doubt and worry about never finding the love we all so desperately desire. In *The Love Everybody Wants*, Madi shares a revelation that changed her life: *The love we're all searching for is already ours.*

Learn more about Madison's books at waterbrookmultnomah.com.

Listen to Madi's Podcast

STAY TRUE